You and Your Child

BIBLE STUDY GUIDE

From the Bible-teaching ministry of

Charles R. Swindoll

INSIGHT FOR LIVING

Charles R. Swindoll is a graduate of Dallas Theological Seminary and has served in pastorates for over twenty-three years, including churches in Texas, New England, and California. Since 1971 he has served as senior pastor of the First Evangelical Free Church of Fullerton, California. Chuck's radio program, "Insight for Living," began in 1979. In addition to his church and radio ministries, Chuck has authored twenty-one books and numerous booklets on a variety of subjects.

Based on the outlines of Chuck's sermons, the study guide text is coauthored by Ken Gire, Jr., a graduate of Texas Christian University and Dallas Theological Seminary. The Living Insights are written by Bill Butterworth, a graduate of Florida Bible College, Dallas Theological Seminary, and Florida Atlantic University. Ken Gire, Jr. is presently the associate editor in the educational products department at Insight for Living, and Bill Butterworth is currently the director of counseling ministries.

Editor in Chief:	Cynthia Swindoll
Coauthor of Text:	Ken Gire, Jr.
Author of Living Insights:	Bill Butterworth
Editorial Assistant:	Becky Anderson
Copy Supervisor:	Wendy Jones
Copy Assistants:	Jane Gillis and Delia Gomez
Director, Communications Division:	Carla Beck
Project Supervisor:	Nina Paris
Art Director:	Becky Englund
Production Artist:	Trisha Smith
Typographer:	Bob Haskins
Calligrapher:	Teri Kahan-Stumpf
Cover Photograph:	G. Robert Nease
Production Supervisor:	Deedee Snyder
Printer:	Frye and Smith

Unless otherwise identified, all Scripture references are from the New American Standard Bible, © The Lockman Foundation 1960, 1962, 1963, 1968, 1971, 1972, 1973, 1975, 1977. Used by permission.

ISBN 0-8499-8285-5

Ordering Information

An album that contains fourteen messages on seven cassettes and corresponds to this study guide may be purchased through Insight for Living, Post Office Box 4444, Fullerton, California 92634. For ordering information and a current catalog, please write our offices or call (714) 870-9161.

Canadian residents may obtain a catalog and ordering information through Insight for Living Ministries, Post Office Box 2510, Vancouver, British Columbia, Canada V6B 3W7, (604) 272-5811. Overseas residents should direct their correspondence to our Fullerton office.

If you wish to order by Visa or MasterCard, you are welcome to use our toll-free number, (800) 772-8888, Monday through Friday between the hours of 8:30 A.M. and 4:00 P.M., Pacific time. This number may be used anywhere in the continental United States excluding Alaska, California, and Hawaii. Orders from those areas can be made by calling our general office number, (714) 870-9161.

Table of Contents

Although this study guide corresponds to the *You and Your Child* cassette series, it does not directly correlate with the book *You and Your Child* (Nashville, Tenn.: Thomas Nelson Publishers, 1977). Chuck wrote the book after preaching the initial series and decided to add some helpful material which is not included in the study guide. The following notes indicate how the cassette series and the study guide correspond to the chapters in the book.

1. The subject matter in this lesson corresponds to "Mom and Dad...Meet Your Child," chapter 1 of the book.

2. The subject matter in this lesson corresponds to "You Can't Have One without the Other," chapter 3 of the book.

3. The subject matter in this lesson corresponds to "The Evil Bent," the second half of chapter 2 in the book.

4. The subject matter in this lesson corresponds to "Dealing with Rebellion and Disobedience," chapter 6 in the book.

5. There is no chapter in the book on this subject.

6. The subject matter in this lesson corresponds to "Straight Talk on Survival Training," chapter 4 of the book.

7. The subject matter in this lesson is not included in the book.

Two chapters from the book—chapter 9, "Those Extra-Special Children," and chapter 11, "Hope for the Hurting"—are not included in the study guide. We recommend these chapters for those who are experiencing hurt in their family relationships, or for those who desire insight about extra-special little ones—children who are adopted, handicapped, unplanned, gifted, or hyperactive, or who are from single-parent homes.

You and Your Child

This study is for moms and dads . . . those of us engaged in the exacting and often frustrating task of raising children. If you are like me, you are weary of theories and seminars and sermons that sound good but prove unrealistic.

What we want is reliable direction—useful and dependable principles that work. Our great goal is to launch into society secure, mature, confident, and capable young adults who can handle the pressures thrown at them in the demanding arena of life. The home—not the school or the church—is the cutting edge of that process. Home is where the rubber meets the road, where our children are prepared for the future.

Our prime source of information comes from the One who originated the whole idea of home and family . . . God Himself. I have simply taken some of the truths He has preserved for us in the Old and New Testaments and applied them to the task of raising children today. God is the One who brought you and your child together, and He will provide you with the daily wisdom you need to raise your child successfully.

Chuck Swindoll

Chuck Swindoll

Putting Truth into Action

Knowledge apart from application falls short of God's desire for His children. Knowledge must result in change and growth. Consequently, we have constructed this Bible study guide with these purposes in mind: (1) to stimulate discovery, (2) to increase understanding, and (3) to encourage application.

At the end of each lesson is a section called **Living Insights.** *There you'll be given assistance in further Bible study, thoughtful interaction, and personal appropriation. This is the place where the lesson is fitted with shoe leather for your walk through the varied experiences of life.*

It's our hope that you'll discover numerous ways to use this tool. Some useful avenues we would suggest are personal meditation, joint discovery, and discussion with your spouse, family, work associates, friends, or neighbors. The study guide is also practical for church classes and, of course, as a study aid for the "Insight for Living" radio broadcast. The individual studies can usually be completed in thirty minutes. However, some are more open-ended and could be expanded for greater depth. Their use is flexible!

In order to derive the greatest benefit from this process, we suggest that you record your responses to the lessons in a notebook where writing space is plentiful. In view of the kinds of questions asked, your notebook may become a journal filled with your many discoveries and commitments. We anticipate that you will find yourself returning to it periodically for review and encouragement.

Ken Gire, Jr.
Coauthor of Text

Bill Butterworth
Author of Living Insights

You and Your Child

Knowing Your Child
Proverbs 22:6, Psalm 139

Umbilically tied to each newborn bundle brought home from the hospital is a mixed bag of parental emotions ranging anywhere from anticipation to anxiety. Within that bag a nagging question tugs at every parent: "When should I begin to instill Christian character in my child?" The purpose of this study is to demonstrate that the time to begin the child-training process is when you know your child. Because understanding your child is basic if the training is to be effective.

I. Understanding the Training Process

Proverbs 22:6 is key in understanding the process of knowing and raising your child:

> Train up a child in the way he should go,
> Even when he is old he will not depart from it.

A. The popular conception of the training. Many see this verse as meaning that if the child plays the prodigal later on in life and sows his wild oats, at some point, like the prodigal, he'll come to his senses, sober up, shape up, and ship back to God. That is, if he's received the right training as a child. As popular as this interpretation might be, it does not square with Scripture, as we will see, nor does it square with our experience. Experience teaches us that wild oats can make for a painful harvest. Not all prodigals come home. Not all ships return safely to harbor. The bottom of the ocean is strewn with the wreckage of ships that have broken loose from their moorings and strayed from their course, never to return home. You can probably think of numerous examples. People who were forced by the sheer determination and strictness of their parents to be in church every Sunday, to read the Bible every day, to memorize Scripture, to read only "Christian" books, and see only "Christian" films. All this the parent does thinking that the child is being "trained up in the way he should go." Yet, when finally out of the nest, the child stretches his wings, takes off, and throws eggs at everything "Christian." The rebellion is deep-seated and probably

1

aimed not so much at Christianity as it is at the parents who never won the right to be heard and never took the time or trouble to get to *know* their child as a person. Anyone resents being run through an impersonal curriculum and revolts against being treated as a nonperson. Children are no different. At the center of their being, they want to be *known,* intimately and genuinely. For parents of prodigals, this interpretation of Proverbs 22:6 offers little salve. In this bewildering wilderness experience, hope is a distant mirage. Frankly, the verse offers much hope, but a closer look is needed to anchor that hope in reality.

B. The nature of the training. Let's begin by looking at the words *train up.* This term originally referred to "the palate, the roof of the mouth, the gums." In the verbal form, the word was used for breaking a wild horse by placing a rope in its mouth and thereby bringing it into submission. It was also used to describe the action of a midwife, who, soon after helping in the birth of a child, would dip her fingers into the juice of crushed dates, reach into the mouth of the infant, and massage its gums and palate. This tangy taste created a sensation for sucking. Then she would take the child and place it in the mother's arms to begin nursing. So also, the parent is to bring the child into submission and create a thirst for the nourishing flow of the parents' wisdom and counsel.

C. The duration of the training. Two words in verse 6 help survey the parameters of the training in terms of time. The word *child* invariably calls to mind a little one between infancy and four or five years of age. However, the Scriptures use the term in a broader sense, ranging anywhere from a newborn to a person of marriageable age (cf. 1 Sam. 4:20–21, 1:22–23; Gen. 37:2). In the second half of the verse, the root meaning of the Hebrew word for *old* is "bearded" or "chin." Solomon is not envisioning a seventy-year-old prodigal returning home. A boy starts growing a beard on his chin when he approaches maturity. The point is, when the child reaches maturity, he will not depart from the way in which he has been trained. Therefore, the responsibility of the parents is to train up, create a thirst, build into the child this experience of submission, and to continue that training the entire time the child is under their care.

D. The implementation of the training. The manner of training is suggested by the word *in.* The term means "in keeping with, in cooperation with, in accordance to something." The literal rendering is "according to his way." That's altogether different from your way, your plan, your idea, your curriculum. The verse doesn't mean "train up a child as you see him." Rather,

"If you want your training to be meaningful and wise, be observant and discover your child's way, and adapt your training accordingly." Strengthening this idea is the word *way*. This Hebrew term literally means "road" or "path." Metaphorically, it is "a characteristic." Therefore, the thought is, "according to his characteristic, his manner." In Proverbs 22:6, the word *way* is used in the same sense: "Train up a child in keeping with his characteristics." And his characteristics are distinct and set. There is a bent[1] already established within every child God places in our care. Each is not, in fact, a pliable lump of clay but has been bent, prescribed according to a predetermined pattern. For example, perhaps you have several children in your home. If not, perhaps you were from a home of several children. One may be creative; another, practical. One may be intelligent; another, just average. One may be outgoing; another, withdrawn. Whatever the case, they're all individuals. They weren't created on the assembly line. They were handcrafted, individually, by God. Consider Cain and Abel. Different as night and day. One godless; the other, pleasing God. Or Jacob and Esau. Esau was a hunter, manly and hairy. Jacob, a momma's boy. Or how about Absalom and Solomon? Same father, same home environment—yet different. Absalom was a rebel, foolish and impulsive. Solomon was a man of peace, wise and discerning. All are individuals. Each has his own individual bents. The short-sighted parent, however, overlooks this, focusing only on the immediate task of making the children conform, shaping them up. The result? When the parent starts barking "shape up or ship out," the child starts saving up for a boat ticket. Invariably, parents make two common mistakes. First, they use the same approach with all their children. Secondly, they compare them with other children. Both mistakes stem from not knowing them, from failing to see their individual bents. Consequently, the crucial concern for us as parents is to understand what the bents are in each of our children.

Some Personal Application

The point of contact where much family friction generates is the child's perception of himself versus the parents' perception of him. There the conflict begins to heat. Lines are drawn. Sides are taken. Boxing gloves put on. Force is then exerted by a bigger woman—namely Mom—and by

---

1. Psalm 7:12 confirms this usage of a *bent* to describe a "way" or "characteristic." The word *bent* is the verbal form of the word *way* and is here used of God who "has bent His bow and made it ready."

a bigger man—namely Dad. Outnumbered and overpowered, the child feels backed into a corner. Is it any surprise he fights back? Inevitably, what gets beat up is the child's self-worth. A heart God designed to be filled with love and tenderness is now a vacuum where hurt rushes in. Following close behind, grasping hurt's hand, is resentment—and clutching its hand, rebellion. Do your child a favor; take off the gloves, step out of the ring, go out and just talk. And, for a change, let your child do most of the talking. You listen (cf. James 1:19b). It will be a breath of fresh air for you both, and—who knows?—it may become habit-forming.

II. Understanding Your Child's Nature

There are three things revealed in Scripture concerning the bent of every child.

  A. A general bent toward good. Coined in the image of God, the child bears a certain imprint of divinity (Gen. 1:26–27). From this, each person derives a dignity and worth that is to be known and protected (cf. Gen. 9:6, James 3:9). The child also has been given a unique personality and distinctive abilities.

  B. A general bent toward evil. Like Midas in reverse, Adam's touch on us all has turned the luster of God's image into tarnish (Rom. 5:12). Each child, then, to use C. S. Lewis's words, is born a "Son of Adam or Daughter of Eve,"[2] not a child of God. Sin's poison passes from generation to generation through the bloodstream of humanity. As a result, each child's spirit is brought into the world—stillborn. The only remedy is to be " 'born again' " (John 3:3). A paraphrase of Psalm 51:5 exemplifies this bent toward evil: "Behold, I was brought forth in a state of iniquity, / My mother was sinful who conceived me, and I, too, am sinful." Psalm 58:3 conveys the same thought: "The wicked are estranged from the womb; / These who speak lies go astray from birth." Our experience confirms these truths. You have to instruct children to tell the truth, but you never have to sit down and teach them to lie. That's part of their bent. It comes naturally. If you fail to understand this bent toward evil, inherited from Adam, you will fail to understand the spiritual battle in general and your child in particular.

  C. A specific bent toward evil. Aside from their roots in Adam, all children have a specific bent toward evil which is inherited

2. C. S. Lewis, *The Lion, the Witch, and the Wardrobe* (New York: Collier Books, 1970), p. 10.

from their immediate family (Exod. 34:7). In some strange genetics of the soul, sin and its effects pass through the family tree like sap. This will be dealt with in depth in lesson 2.

Some Personal Application

" 'A pupil is not above his teacher; but everyone, after he has been fully trained, will be like his teacher' " (Luke 6:40). In other words, once you've fully trained your child, he's going to be like *you.* Now that's a sobering thought. As much as we sometimes hate to admit it, our children are a reflection of us and of the dynamics at work in our home. Take a good look—an honest, nondefensive look—at your children. What do you see in them that reflects you? Don't you think it would be easier changing *you* than two or three or four of them?

III. Understanding Your Child's Uniqueness
A. The emotional structure of your child is unique.
Psalm 139:13–16 describes the uniqueness God gives to every child before they were ever born.[3] Verse 13: "For Thou didst form my inward parts." *Inward parts,* literally "kidney" in the Hebrew, was used to refer to the emotional structure of the individual, the "seat of the tenderest, most secret emotions."[4] In our culture, the organ of the heart is used in a similar manner.
B. The physical structure of your child is unique. The
writer of the psalm goes on to say, "Thou didst weave me in my mother's womb." The word *weave* means "to knit together into a mass or thicket." With that embryonic ball of yarn, God knits together each child. In the fourteenth verse David praises God upon reflection on this thought. He says, "I will give thanks to Thee, for I am fearfully and wonderfully made." Then, he continues the anatomy lesson in verse 15: "My frame [literally, skeleton, bony structure] was not hidden from Thee, / When I was made in secret, / And skillfully wrought in the depths of the

---

3. In Ecclesiastes, Solomon looks at the development of the child within the womb as one of the great mysteries of life (11:5). Some stunning examples of fiber-optic photography that display the process of development within the womb and illustrate Psalm 139 can be found in the book *A Child Is Born,* by Lennart Nilsson (New York: Delacorte Press, 1977). For illustrations and spiritual applications of Psalm 139 from a surgeon's perspective, consult *Fearfully and Wonderfully Made,* by Dr. Paul Brand and Philip Yancey (Grand Rapids, Mich.: Zondervan Publishing House, 1980). For a parallel passage to Psalm 139, see Job 10:8–11.

4. C. F. Keil and F. Delitzsch, *Commentary on the Old Testament in Ten Volumes,* vol. 5: *Psalms,* by F. Delitzsch (Grand Rapids, Mich.: William B. Eerdmans Publishing Company, 1982), p. 349. Both the "kidneys" and the "heart" are tried by God (Ps. 7:9).

earth." The word translated *skillfully wrought* is used in Exodus to describe the curtains for the Tabernacle. They were to be made and fitted, formed and embroidered together so that the tapestry reveals beauty. Like fine needlepoint, God put us together. *In secret, in the depths of the earth* is an idiom for "a place of protection, concealment." It's a figurative, poetic way of describing the womb. In that protected and concealed place, God oversaw our prenatal development.

C. The structure of your child's life span is unique.
Verse 16 states, "Thine eyes have seen my unformed substance." *Unformed substance* is used in the Talmud to indicate every kind of as yet unshapen stuff and raw material, like a block of wood or lump of clay. When applied to a human vessel, it would be equivalent to "embryo." The word *seen* means "watched over" in an active sense—as architects painstakingly watch over the construction of a building they have drawn. God had a plan in His mind for the child and watches over that gestation period to the extent that even the days of his life are prescribed: "And in Thy book they were all written, / The days that were ordained for me, / When as yet there was not one of them" (v. 16).

Some Personal Application

The psalmist wants you to realize that the sovereign God of heaven has given you a very special gift. He has planned and arranged your child to be a certain way, with a specific set of attributes and abilities, and a unique personality—and a specific limit to the days your child has allotted to spend on this earth. Make the most of those days, won't you? Get started on the right foot and get to *know* the child God has so graciously entrusted to you.

🔥 *Living Insights*

When God deposits a child into a parent's arms, the newborn comes with a distinct individuality, or what we are calling a *bent*. The Bible is filled with examples of this prescribed individuality. Copy the following list of biblical characters in your own study notebook. Next to each name, jot down a word or phrase that best describes your recollection of the person's individuality. After the list is complete, return to the key passages of Scripture on each person, and check out how well you did in your description!

- Cain (Genesis 4) _____
- Abel (Genesis 4) _____
- Jacob (Genesis 25–27) _____
- Esau (Genesis 25–27) _____
- Solomon (2 Samuel 12–15) _____
- Absalom (2 Samuel 12–15) _____
- Isaac (Genesis 16–22) _____
- Ishmael (Genesis 16–22) _____
- Samuel (1 Samuel 1–3) _____
- Moses (Exodus 1–2) _____
- Samson (Judges 13–14) _____
- Joseph (Genesis 37–39) _____

🔥 *Living Insights*

The key application of this first lesson is the importance of knowing your child. If you're a parent, construct the following chart for each of your children (one chart per child). If possible, sit down with your mate and discuss each child's individual makeup. If you're not a parent, do this exercise for yourself and your brothers/sisters.

Child's Name: _____	
Evidences of a Bad Bent	Evidences of a Good Bent

Breaking Granddad's Bent

Exodus 34:5–8

Physicians tell us that diseases and physical maladies are often passed down from one generation to another. Psychiatrists inform us that mental illnesses and emotional disturbances are often hereditary. It stands to reason that if this is true in the physical, mental, and emotional realms, it is true in the spiritual realm as well. From generation to generation we pass down an inheritance of characteristics, both physical and nonphysical. As there is a genetics of the cell, so there is a genetics of the soul. With regard to the latter, there are three major aspects concerning our heritage. First, every person is born in the image of God,[1] along with a God-given personality and distinct abilities. Second, every person is born with a sin nature, a general bent toward evil, inherited from Adam (Rom. 5:12, 3:10–12). In this study we're going to explore the third area—a specific bent toward evil inherited from our more immediate forefathers and its resultant consequences.

I. The Consequences of Inherited Sin

In Exodus 34:5–8, amid the clefts of Mount Sinai, Moses brushes with the glory of God in an awesome daybreak encounter. Cloaked in a cloud of mystery, God pierces the thin mountain air with an incisive revelation about His character:

> And the Lord descended in the cloud and stood there with him as he called upon the name of the Lord. Then the Lord passed by in front of him and proclaimed, "The Lord, the Lord God, compassionate and gracious, slow to anger, and abounding in lovingkindness and truth; who keeps lovingkindness for thousands, who forgives iniquity, transgression and sin; yet He will by no means leave the guilty unpunished, visiting the iniquity of fathers on the children and on the grandchildren to the third and fourth generations." And Moses made haste to bow low toward the earth and worship.

---

1. Relevant passages on man as the image of God are Genesis 1:26–27; 5:1, 3; 9:6; 1 Corinthians 11:7; Colossians 3:10; and James 3:9. Psalm 8, although not containing the words *image of God,* deals with the creation of man and his dominion over the earth (see also Heb. 2:6–8). The New Testament views Jesus as the image of God *par excellence* (cf. 2 Cor. 4:4, Col. 1:15, Heb. 1:2–3). And when we become united with Jesus by faith, the Father commences our restoration into the image of Christ (Rom. 8:29, 2 Cor. 3:18, Eph. 4:24, Col. 3:10). For an account of the historical debates concerning the *image of God,* see G. C. Berkouwer, *Man: The Image of God,* trans. D. Jellema (Grand Rapids, Mich.: William B. Eerdmans Publishing Co., 1962), especially chapter 2. For an insightful exegetical study, consult Henri Blocher, *In the Beginning,* trans. David G. Preston (Downers Grove, Ill.: InterVarsity Press, 1984), pp. 79–94. For a comprehensive, yet succinct study on this topic, see Charles Lee Feinberg, "The Image of God," *Bibliotheca Sacra,* 129:515 (July–Sept. 1972), pp. 235–46.

The latter half of verse 7 is the foreboding edge of the revelation which glints in the morning sun and catches our eye: "Visiting the iniquity of fathers on the children and on the grandchildren to the third and fourth generations."[2] The term *iniquity* is taken from the Hebrew word meaning "to bend, to twist, to distort, to pervert" (cf. Prov. 12:8, where it is translated "perverse"). Consequently, the amplified translation would read, "Visiting the bent, the twisting distortions, the perversions of the fathers on the children and on the grandchildren to the third and fourth generations." At first glance this seems vengeful and unfair. Yet the opposite is true. God could have allowed that same perversion or bent to continue throughout the family's history so that the growing problem would end up fraying the family line. Then, no thread would escape the abrasive stone of His judgment. But God says, "No. It will be visited to the third and fourth generations." The scales are weighted not on God's harshness but on His kindness. Judgment will extend to only three or four generations. However, His loyal and merciful love—"loving-kindness"—will extend to thousands. He will forgive iniquity, transgression, and sin if and when it is dealt with. If confessed, there is cleansing (1 John 1:9). If not, a terrible price will be exacted, and God will mete out the punishment in installments to the children and the children's children. Proverbs 28:13 instructs us that the response we have to our own sin tips the balance as to whether justice or mercy will be measured out to us: "He who conceals his transgressions will not prosper, / But he who confesses and forsakes them will find compassion." The sickle of God cuts a swath of judgment through the rampant overgrowth of sin. We'll trek first through a wide swing of Israel's history, then through a narrower stroke in the life and lineage of Abraham.

II. A General Example of Inherited Sin

The historical books of Kings and Chronicles document the civil war that split the nation of Israel into two kingdoms. The southern kingdom was ruled by Rehoboam, Solomon's son. The reins to the northern kingdom were wrested by the wicked Jeroboam, Solomon's other son, who spurred the nation on to runaway sinfulness. Twenty-one times in Kings and Chronicles we read that the nation walked "in the way of Jeroboam" (cf. 1 Kings 15:34, 16:26). Jeroboam's followers picked up his sins of idolatry, sexual immorality, and rebellion. Like polluted tributaries, these three bents filled the history of the nation to the saturation point of God's wrath until, at last, judgment rained on them in the form of foreign

---

2. The identical phrase was first introduced in the giving of the Ten Commandments in Exodus 20:5.

domination.[3] Turning back the pages of time, we'll now examine a more specific trail of inherited sin.

III. A Specific Example of Inherited Sin

The family is Abraham's. The bent is lying.

A. In Abraham's life. Abraham's deception rears its cowardly head in Genesis 20:

> Now Abraham journeyed from there toward the land of the Negev, and settled between Kadesh and Shur; then he sojourned in Gerar. And Abraham said of Sarah his wife, "She is my sister." So Abimelech king of Gerar sent and took Sarah. But God came to Abimelech in a dream of the night, and said to him, "Behold, you are a dead man because of the woman whom you have taken, for she is married." Now Abimelech had not come near her; and he said, "Lord, wilt Thou slay a nation, even though blameless? Did he not himself say to me, 'She is my sister'? And she herself said, 'He is my brother.' In the integrity of my heart and the innocence of my hands I have done this." (vv. 1–7)

Pardoning, God eases the snare off Abimelech (vv. 6–8), after which the ruffled and flustered king tracks Abraham down to demand an explanation:

> Then Abimelech called Abraham and said to him, "What have you done to us? And how have I sinned against you, that you have brought on me and on my kingdom a great sin? You have done to me things that ought not to be done." And Abimelech said to Abraham, "What have you encountered, that you have done this thing?" (vv. 9–10)

Abraham responds by tailoring a hasty rationalization into a loose-fitting apology:

> "Because I thought, surely there is no fear of God in this place; and they will kill me because of my wife. Besides, she actually is my sister, the daughter of my father, but not the daughter of my mother, and she became my wife; and it came about, when God caused me to wander from my father's house, that I said to her, 'This is the kindness which you will show

---

3. Twice the Assyrians conquered the northern kingdom—Israel—the most noted occasion being the fall of Samaria (722/3 B.C.). The southern kingdom—Judah—was conquered once by Assyria and three times by the Babylonians, the most noted time being the fall of Jerusalem (586 B.C.). Each time, the conquerors took back with them a host of Jewish captives. For further reference, consult *The Bible Almanac,* ed. James I. Packer, Merrill C. Tenney, and William White, Jr. (Nashville: Thomas Nelson Publishers, 1980), pp. 33–36.

to me: everywhere we go, say of me, "He is my brother." ' " (vv. 11–13)

Abraham's line of reasoning was that since Sarah was his father's daughter from another marriage, his half-sister, there was truth in what he said. But his statement implied something that was absolutely false. She was not only his sister; she was also his wife. His intent was to mislead Abimelech. In an earlier chapter in Abraham's life, we find that lying is a definite, unchecked weakness in his character (Gen. 12:10–20). It is hardly a flattering portrait these two passages paint of the pillar of faith and founding father of Israel. But like Chaucer's *Canterbury Tales* where the Miller's nose is distinguished by a prominent wart, Scripture sketches its heroes . . . blemishes and all.

> **A Thought to Consider**
> "All truth is safe and nothing else is safe; and he who keeps back the truth, or withholds it from men, from motives of expedience, is either a coward or a criminal, or both."[4]

B. In Isaac's life. The bent of lying surfaces in Isaac's life through a situation similar to the one his father had experienced years earlier. As we read the account in Genesis 26:6–11, we can't help but think, "like father, like son." The same bent that was not straightened out in Abraham's life resurfaced in the life of his son. From there, because unchecked, it passed to Isaac's son Jacob.

C. In Jacob's life. Isaac and his wife Rebekah had two sons, Jacob and Esau. Esau was an outdoorsman, a hunter, and was favored by his father. Jacob "lived in tents," was a "peaceful man," and was undoubtedly "Momma's boy." It doesn't take much imagination to visualize the conflicts. At an early age Jacob began to develop a habit of deception, seeing that it would help him gain the advantage he needed to get ahead in life. Encouraged by his mother, this habit culminated in a treacherous act of deception. Genesis 25:27–33 gives an account of Jacob[5] bartering the birthright away from his older twin. In his dying days, Isaac summons the older Esau to go into the field, hunt game, and prepare a last meal for him so "that I may eat, so that my soul may bless you before I die" (27:1–4). Rebekah overhears this, conspires with Jacob, and they plot to take

4. Max Muller, quoted in *Speaker's Encyclopedia of Stories, Quotes, and Anecdotes,* compiled by Jacob M. Braude (Englewood Cliffs, N.J.: Prentice-Hall, 1966), p. 393.

5. Jacob's name literally means "supplanter." *Webster's New Universal Unabridged Dictionary* defines *supplant* as "to take the place of; supersede, especially through force, scheming, or treachery."

advantage of Isaac's poor eyesight and Esau's absence in the field (vv. 5–17). In an act of deception and lying, Jacob masquerades as his brother and obtains the blessing for himself (vv. 18–29). With faint eyesight and probably hearing, too, Isaac asks, "Are you really my son Esau?" And he said, "I am" (v. 24). There's the lie, as bold and brazen as it can be. And so deception continues to unravel Abraham's tight-knit family until it is a snarl of tangled values and relationships.

D. In Jacob's sons. Like a submerged air bubble racing to the water's surface, the irrepressible buoyancy of this character trait causes it to pop up in the lives of Jacob's twelve sons. Like his parents, he, too, had his favorites, the foremost being Joseph. However, the other sons resented their brother. The story in Genesis 37 records the jealous dispute over the interpretation of a dream Joseph had. The other brothers decide to put him in a cistern, a cavernous desert well, where he is picked up by a slave caravan and ends up in bondage in Egypt. To cover the crime, Jacob's sons take Joseph's distinctive, multi-colored garment, dip it in animal's blood, and bring it back to their father, explaining, "We found this; please examine it to see whether it is your son's tunic or not" (v. 32). That was the spoken lie. They hadn't found it. The whole scene, props and all, was staged. The second lie was unspoken. Jacob examined the garment and said: "It is my son's tunic. A wild beast has devoured him; Joseph has surely been torn to pieces!" (v. 33). They didn't say a word, but by their silence they lied. Like father, like sons.

> **A Thought to Consider**
> "It is all in vain to preach the truth,
> To the eager ears of a trusting youth,
> If, whenever the lad is standing by,
> He sees you cheat and he hears you lie."[6]

IV. Short-Circuiting the Consequences of Inherited Sin

By now, you're probably asking yourself how you can trip the breaker on those bents and short-circuit the process at work in your own family. There are several steps you can take to help your children come to terms with their character bents.

A. Introduce your child to Jesus Christ. The first and biggest step to straighten out the bents is for the child to become aligned to Him who is "the way, and the truth, and the life" (John 14:6).

---

6. Edgar A. Guest, from his poem "Hypocrisy," quoted in *Speaker's Encyclopedia*, p. 185.

B. Pray for insight into your child's character. Remember, to a large degree, your child is a reflection of you. Insight into your character may lead to insight into your child (cf. Ps. 139:23–24).

C. Become a student of your child. Stop. Look. Listen. Pay close attention to the actions (1 Tim. 5:25, Gal. 5:19) and words (Luke 6:45) which reflect inner character.

D. Be consistent. Consistency is what molds character over the long haul.

E. Maintain open and loving communication with your family. You will never know your child unless you take control of your schedule and plan time to listen and observe. This may necessitate putting the TV to bed early instead of the children. Or how about taking your child with you to work one day instead of bringing your work home? Whatever it takes, your child is worth it!

🔥 *Living Insights*

Study One ━━━━━━━━━━━━━━━━━━━━━━━━━━

The thrust of this study is Exodus 34:7. At first glance, this verse may seem harsh and unfair. But when you study it carefully in its context, the opposite you will find to be true.

● Copy the following chart in your notebook. The left column contains key words from Exodus 34:7. In the center column, write a definition for each word. Finally, use the right column for a statement concerning the significance of the word.

Exodus 34:7—A Closer Look		
Terms	Meanings	Importance
lovingkindness		
iniquity		
transgression		
sin		
unpunished		
fathers		
children		
grandchildren		
generations		

Continued on next page

13

Living Insights

Your child has a bent . . . are you aware of it? How well do you know your child? Take some time to answer those questions by filling in a report card on your parental activities. Read each statement, grade yourself (A + through F), and write the reason for the grade. Remember, do one card per child.

PARENTAL REPORT CARD		
SUBJECT	GRADE	REASON
Introducing Your Child to Christ		
Praying for Your Child		
Studying Your Child		
Consistency with Your Child		
Communicating with Your Child		

GRADING SYSTEM

A—Excellent   B—Above Average   C—Average   D—Below Average   F—Failing

Loving Your Child
Psalms 127–128

When we visit places like museums or historical sites, we often notice murals in which the artist has chronicled the significant events of a single war, a monarchy, or an entire era. As we walk along and observe the painting, we pass year after year in the history of the artist's subject. Similarly, Psalms 127 and 128 form a beautiful, domestic mural, unrolling before our eyes the development of a happy and healthy home.

I. A Panoramic View

Let's begin our study by first taking a step or two back to appreciate the scope of the artist's work. The first brush strokes of Psalm 127 portray the home in its early, spring years. The proper foundation for the home is a trust in the Lord to build, protect, and bless the family. An illustration of that blessing is seen in the gift of children (vv. 3–5). Then in Psalm 128:1–3, we see something of the training that takes place in the home. The vitality of those children and of those relationships within the home (vv. 2–3) are a direct result of God's blessing, which flows from the parents' relationship and obedience to the Lord (vv. 1, 4). As we come to the end of our mural, the muted colors of autumn years tint the last two verses of the psalm. However, gilding the edges of the falling leaves is the rejuvenating blessing of grandchildren.

II. A Probing Close-Up

Now we'll take several steps closer and scrutinize each scene. The first two verses of Psalm 127 are the piers and beams of the home, the foundation from which all else derives its stability and security.

Unless the Lord builds the house,
They labor in vain who build it;
Unless the Lord guards the city,
The watchman keeps awake in vain. (v. 1)

Solomon, the writer of this psalm, compares the home to a city. When an ancient city was built, it was not uncommon for its walls to be finished first to keep out the enemy. If the people trusted in the walls to protect them, to give them security, their trust was misplaced, creating only a false sense of security. Likewise, walls we erect around our families and possessions offer only an illusion of security. Like Jericho's walls, they can tumble as quickly as a shout. For ultimately, it is not the watchman or the walls that protect the city; it is the *Lord.* "The name of the Lord is a strong tower; / The righteous runs into it and is safe" (Prov. 18:10). In the same sense, unless a husband and wife trust in God, their work and their watchfulness is wasted.

In verse 2, Solomon qualifies the phrase *in vain:*
> It is vain for you to rise up early,
> To retire late,
> To eat the bread of painful labors.

Many feel that by working longer hours they can provide more things
to bring happiness to their home or afford a nicer, newer home in
hopes that it will bring happiness. That's the "bread of painful labors." And it doesn't satisfy that empty longing in the pit of our soul,
that longing for a home, a *real* home—a home where love thrives,
lush and fragrant. The reason why it's futile burning the candle at
both ends—rising early, retiring late—is that God, not our labors,
is the source of our blessing, as verse 2 indicates: "For He gives to
His beloved even in his sleep." A perfect example of His giving is
found in verses 3–5: our own children. There are four metaphors
Solomon uses to describe children. Each is worth noting.

A. Children are a gift. "Children are a gift of the Lord" (v. 3a).
The Hebrew word for *gift* means "property" or "possession."
Your children are God's property, which He has entrusted to you.

B. Children are a reward. "The fruit of the womb is a reward"
(v. 3b). In an ultimate sense, it is bestowed because of the parents' love for the Lord and their trust in Him who "builds the

house" and "guards the city." In an immediate sense, it is a reward God bestows on the loving commitment between a man and a woman. God begins a process at conception to design and construct a visual aid of their love. And that bundle of animation is given to the couple as a prize, a trophy, a reward of their love and trust.

C. Children are arrows. Consider the verses which follow:

Like arrows in the hand of a warrior,
So are the children of one's youth.
How blessed is the man whose quiver is full of them;
They shall not be ashamed,
When they speak with their enemies in the gate.
(vv. 4–5)

The word *arrows* paints a picture of the strength and security that children provide for their parents (cf. 1 Tim. 5:4). However, a dull or bent arrow offers little hope in battle. Skill in handling the arrow is also of utmost importance—the amount of tension on the bow, the position of your arms and shoulders, where you fix your eyes in relation to the tip of the arrow, the release. It's an exacting skill.

A Personal Application

Into your quiver God has placed particularly designed, prescribed arrows. They will, by the wise parent, be drawn out, examined, and understood—*before* they are launched into the world. Child-rearing, like archery, is difficult to master. After all, if it were easy, the process would have never started with something called "labor"! Children are arrows in your quiver, but are your hands "the hands of a warrior"—steady, strong, and skilled?

D. Children are olive plants. In verses 1–3 of Psalm 128, we find the fourth description of children. Solomon sets a table that would have been the envy of Norman Rockwell:

How blessed is everyone who fears the Lord,
Who walks in His ways.
When you shall eat of the fruit of your hands,
You will be happy and it will be well with you.
Your wife shall be like a fruitful vine,
Within your house,
Your children like olive plants
Around your table.

The original Hebrew text reads, "Your children will be like transplanted olive branches." Notice the word *transplanted.* You see,

17

God had this seed which He designed and prepared and made sure had a safe greenhouse in which to develop for nine months. At the end of this time, He deposited into your hands a tender, little transplanted olive plant which was your child. So your children sit around your table where your wife, like a fruit-bearing vine, entwines herself. What a beautiful setting—so tender, so vibrant, so perfectly arranged!

III. A Prescription

Having considered these four descriptions, let's turn our attention to what our response should be to these new insights about our children.

A. **Appreciate the gift.** If you really see your children as a gift from the Lord, *it should completely change your attitudes* about them. The attitudes should include *awe*—that God would think enough of you to give a gift in the first place—and *appreciation* for the gift itself. Are those your attitudes?

B. **Prize the reward.** Do you really see your children as a reward or a trophy to be displayed with honor? Do your children see satisfaction in your eyes when you look at them? Do you honor them by listening to them and valuing what they think and say and feel? Does your conversation reflect that they are prized?

C. **Develop the arrow.** How are you preparing to send your arrows out into the world? Are they sharp, straight, and true? Or are they dull and bent?

D. **Nurture and prune the olive plants.** Encouragement and discipline, like nurturing and pruning, require plenty of tender, loving care if they are to be effective. Certainly we *all* need pruning from time to time (Heb. 12:5–12, cf. Prov. 13:24); however, you don't club an olive plant with a two-by-four to do it. You prune it with the tenderness of a caring vinedresser and always with the goal in mind of enhancing its ability to bear fruit (John 15:2).

![icon] Living Insights

We cannot love someone we do not know. Hopefully, the first two lessons have given you some tools to better know your child. Let's turn our attention to Psalms 127 and 128 in order to lay the groundwork for loving our children.

- An exciting method of personal Bible study is the art of paraphrasing. Let's apply this approach to Psalms 127–128. Write out these eleven verses in your own words. In doing so, seek to bring out the feelings and meanings that are "between the lines" of these poetic phrases. Ask God to give you something special from this text.

![icon] Living Insights

How well do you know your child? How much do you love your child? There is an expert in these areas . . . your child! Are you brave enough to sit down and talk with your expert? Arrange for a special, quiet time alone with your child. After you've small-talked and gained a measure of comfort, ask the following questions—and be ready for some honest answers!

- Do Mom and Dad really listen to you?
- Are Mom and Dad courteous in the way we talk with you?
- What do you think of the discipline in our home?
- How do you feel about the amount of time we spend with you?

You Can't Have One without the Other

Selected Proverbs

Dr. Rene Spitz, a New York City physician, reported on a test conducted a number of years ago in South America. The results have since been published in several medical and educational journals.[1] The test was conducted on 239 institutionalized children, over a period of five years. The children were confined in two different environments and were studied simultaneously. Both institutions were equivalent in all physical respects, including housing, food, and hygienic standards. The institutions differed in but one factor—the amount of loving affection provided. The contrast in results was dramatic. In "Nursery" the children, placed there three months after birth, showed normal development, some even above average, according to Dr. Spitz. But after two years in "Foundling Home," where there was no show of love, the emotionally starved children were not able to speak, walk, or feed themselves. With one or two exceptions in a total of ninety-one children, those who survived were human wrecks. The mortality rate was equally startling. In "Nursery" not one child was lost through death. In "Foundling Home" there was a 37 percent mortality rate. Although we believe the nature of this test to be a blatant disregard for the sanctity of human life and goes beyond the ethical bounds of science, we can learn something from the results. In a very real sense, we love or we perish. Love is essential for human development, and it is essential for a happy, healthy home. You can't have one without the other. The absence of love or the wrong type of love in a home can produce heart-breaking results.

I. Some Selective Parents

A case in point is the relationship of two parents, Isaac and Rebekah, toward their sons, Jacob and Esau. Isaac and Rebekah were equally to blame in "training up" their children poorly, because they were selective in their love and in their loyalties to them.

A. Selective in their love. Genesis 25 records the births of Jacob and Esau along with the feeling each parent had for them:

And Isaac prayed to the Lord on behalf of his wife, because she was barren; and the Lord answered him and Rebekah his wife conceived. But the children struggled together within her; and she said, "If it is so, why then am I this way?" So she went to inquire of the Lord. And the Lord said to her,

"Two nations are in your womb;
And two peoples shall be separated from
your body;

1. Dr. Rene Spitz, "A Scientist Looks at LOVE," *Phi Delta Kappan* (May 1970), pp. 464–65.

> And one people shall be stronger than the
> other;
> And the older shall serve the younger."
> When her days to be delivered were fulfilled, behold,
> there were twins in her womb. Now the first came
> forth red, all over like a hairy garment; and they
> named him Esau. And afterward his brother came
> forth with his hand holding on to Esau's heel, so his
> name was called Jacob; and Isaac was sixty years old
> when she gave birth to them. When the boys grew
> up, Esau became a skillful hunter, a man of the field;
> but Jacob was a peaceful man, living in tents. Now
> Isaac loved Esau, because he had a taste for game;
> but Rebekah loved Jacob. (vv. 21–28)

Isaac loved Esau because the boy was like himself. In verse 28, the word *because* reveals volumes about Isaac's love for Esau. It was *conditioned* on sharing a mutual interest (cf. v. 27 with 27:3–4). This was a boy with whom he could share his love for the outdoors. They could hunt, camp out, and fish together. But Jacob—well, Jacob liked to stay out of the sun and hang around the tents. Besides, the boy couldn't stand the fierceness of the hunt or the sight of blood—he was "a peaceful man" (v. 27). This is probably why Rebekah's love gravitated toward Jacob. He was around a lot, shared in domestic chores, and was gentle. He appreciated her. Probably, too, Isaac's love for Esau was obvious, and she overcompensated for this with Jacob. Possibly, because Esau was the stronger, the most likely to succeed, she became overprotective and continually rallied for the underdog. Regardless of the motivation, her love did not have an unconditional quality, but rather, an overprotective quality.

B. Selective in their loyalties. The loyalties Isaac and Rebekah had for their children can be seen most especially in times of family conflict. The earliest recorded conflict between the brothers sparks when Jacob takes advantage of Esau by manipulating him out of his birthright (Gen. 25:29–34).[2] As the birthright changes hands, what is really bartered away is each man's character. Jacob, in the buying, demonstrated that he valued spiritual privileges and blessings, but that he was willing to have them only on his terms rather than God's. In contrast, Esau, in the selling, demonstrated that his desire for physical

---

2. The birthright involved "paternal blessing and the place as head of the family; . . . the honor of being in the promised line out of which the Messiah should come; . . . [and] the exercise of the family priesthood" (*The New Unger's Bible Handbook,* by Merrill F. Unger, rev. by Gary N. Larson [Chicago: Moody Press, 1984], p. 55).

gratification overshadowed the value he placed on spiritual things. Then, with a final slurp of Jacob's stew and a backward wipe of his hand over his mouth, and without any recorded show of remorse, he "rose and went on his way. Thus Esau despised his birthright" (v. 34). You can't admire Esau for his expedient values, nor can you respect Jacob for his ruthless cunning. Neither can you turn a critical eye away from the parents whose character blushes in their failure to intervene. Most probably, Rebekah didn't intervene because Jacob, her underdog favorite, had won out. Maybe, by some contorted rationalization, she thought Jacob's actions only helped fulfill God's prophecy about the two boys (v. 23). On the other hand, Isaac might not have stepped in because he thought that *a deal was a deal* and that *a man doesn't go back on his oath*. Of course, this doesn't take into account that the oath was squeezed out of him in duress and at the twist of a chiseler's hands. And, equally plausible, Isaac might not have intervened because of the undue control his wife exerted over him. Sometime later, when Jacob is forty, he takes a walk on the wild side and marries not one, but two, Hittite women, and they made life miserable for Isaac and Rebekah (Gen. 26:34–35). Then in chapter 27, Rebekah and Jacob conspire to deceive Isaac out of giving Esau his rightful blessing as firstborn. This results in a plot on Esau's behalf to kill Jacob after their father passes away (v. 41). This is hardly the picture of the happy, healthy home found in Psalms 127–128. The relationships in this home were a seething cauldron of hatred and deception. It was enough to give a parent ulcers. Apparently, this is how it affected Rebekah:

> And Rebekah said to Isaac, "I am tired of living because of the daughters of Heth; if Jacob takes a wife from the daughters of Heth, like these, from the daughters of the land, what good will my life be to me?" (Gen. 27:46)

Esau probably took the Canaanite wives as an affront to his parents when he finally realized the fraudulent nature of their love. Rebekah's love, if any, was feigned. Isaac's was conditional. Neither loved him simply because he was their child. Neither sought to know him, understand him, or patiently "train him up according to his character" by nurturing the good and pruning back the evil. When Esau was old enough to perceive this, he rebelled. Jacob, on the other hand, for whatever reasons— expedience or obedience—honors his parents' wish by not marrying one of the Canaanite women and seeks a wife of the same bloodline. Meanwhile, Esau, his anger subsiding and his longing to be loved surfacing, sees all this and makes a final lunge at winning his father's approval by taking a wife from one of Abraham's descendants:

> So Esau saw that the daughters of Canaan displeased his father Isaac; and Esau went to Ishmael, and married, besides the wives that he had, Mahalath the daughter of Ishmael, Abraham's son, the sister of Nebaioth. (28:8–9)

This incident illustrates that parental approval is a strong motivation even after the child is grown. And, in the final analysis, children seek from their parents only what the parents themselves long for—to be known intimately, to be accepted fully, and to be loved genuinely. When those needs go unmet in the child, rebellion forms a bitter root in a heart that was once tender. Where love is absent, hatred takes root.

II. Some Selected Proverbs

As preventative medicine, some selected proverbs are provided below for the good health of your home. Notice the contrast between *love* and *hate* as you read.

A. Proverbs 10:12.

> Hatred stirs up strife,
> But love covers all transgressions.

If you seek love in your home, you will do everything possible to handle a conflict without strife—*everything!* As a practical application, stand under the yardstick of 1 Corinthians 13:4–8a to measure how you're growing in this regard.

B. Proverbs 13:24.

> He who spares his rod hates his son,
> But he who loves him disciplines him diligently.

You don't show your love by indifference or negligence but by your *diligence.*

C. Proverbs 15:17.

> Better is a dish of vegetables where love is,
> Than a fattened ox and hatred with it.

By nomadic standards, Jacob and Esau grew up in a prosperous home. But hatred basted the succulent ox and permeated every bite of every meal at every family get-together. Doubtless, looking back, they would have rather had the love, with a dish of vegetables on the side. And so would all children gladly trade all the cold, lifeless, material things they own for a home where love wraps its arms around them and smiles with kind, accepting eyes.

III. Some Before and After Pictures

If your home is already in shambles, and you're far beyond the preventative stage, it's never too late for God to do a complete remodeling job. A before and after picture in Israel's history should give you some encouraging ideas for your house plans.

A. The before: Israel's destruction. In Joel 1, the prophet describes an unprecedented locust plague which was to take place in Israel and prefigure a future judgment on the nation. The land would become completely devastated:

> What the gnawing locust has left, the swarming
> locust has eaten;
> And what the swarming locust has left, the creeping
> locust has eaten;
> And what the creeping locust has left, the stripping
> locust has eaten....
> It has made my vine a waste,
> And my fig tree splinters.
> It has stripped them bare and cast them away;
> Their branches have become white....
> The seeds shrivel under their clods;
> The storehouses are desolate,
> The barns are torn down,
> For the grain is dried up. (vv. 4, 7, 17)

Is that a picture of your home? Are those tender olive plants around your table stripped of their self-esteem? Are there nubs where feelings once were? Are the emotional cupboards in your home empty? Are the rooms chilled with indifference and hate?

B. The after: Israel's restoration. If Joel 1 is a picture of your home, as stark and stripped as it may appear, it is not without hope. In Joel 2, the prophet snaps a prophetic picture, still to be developed, of how God will restore Israel:

> "Then I will make up to you for the years
> That the swarming locust has eaten,
> The creeping locust, the stripping locust, and the
> gnawing locust,
> My great army which I sent among you.
> And you shall have plenty to eat and be satisfied,
> And praise the name of the Lord your God,
> Who has dealt wondrously with you;
> Then My people will never be put to shame.
> Thus you will know that I am in the midst of Israel,
> And that I am the Lord your God
> And there is no other;
> And My people will never be put to shame."
> (vv. 25–27)

He can do that for your home. He can do that for your marriage. He can do that for your children. But first, you need to do an about-face. Before there can be restoration, there must be a return:

"Return to Me with all your heart,
And with fasting, weeping, and mourning;
And rend your heart and not your garments."
Now return to the Lord your God,
For He is gracious and compassionate,
Slow to anger, abounding in lovingkindness,
And relenting of evil. (Joel 2:12–13)

Now there's a picture worth framing—and hanging on your heart!

Living Insights

Study One ▬▬▬▬▬▬▬▬▬▬▬▬▬▬▬▬▬▬▬▬▬▬▬

The old song lyric is true: "You can't have one without the other!" You cannot have a healthy home without love. A statement of that magnitude invites further consideration from a scriptural perspective. What is biblical love, anyway?

● Sixteen descriptions of love can be found in 1 Corinthians 13:4–8. Make a copy of the following chart in your notebook. Begin your study by listing the sixteen words or phrases describing love. Use the center column to jot down other verses or passages of Scripture pertaining to this same concept. Then, use the right column to answer this question: Based on these verses, why is this description of love important?

What Is Biblical Love?		
Description	Cross-references	Importance

Continued on next page

Living Insights

Real love includes involvement. Support and love are meant to be unconditional. Allow the following questions to prod you toward a better understanding of this key issue in parenting.

- What "conditions" do I tend to put on my love?
- How can I express love in a more unconditional manner?
- In what areas is my love tending towards apathy and uninvolvement?
- What are some specific steps I can take in order to express an *involved* love?
- When does my love break down due to my failure to give support?
- What are some practical ways I can be supportive?

Disciplining Your Child

Selected Proverbs

To spank or not to spank—that is *not* the biblical question. The question is *when* and *how* to discipline your child. *When* is discipline appropriate? *How* do you discipline without damaging the child's self-esteem? According to psychologist Dr. James Dobson, "a spanking is to be reserved for use in response to willful defiance, *whenever it occurs.*"[1] Whenever the parent is challenged defiantly, it is important to win that battle the child chooses to initiate. But *how* you triumph over the child's defiance is of utmost importance. Even in a young child, the will is an iron beam within the structure of the human personality. Yet, the will is malleable. It can be molded and polished. In contrast, the child's spirit is a fragile vase. As it relates to the child's sense of personal worth, it can be chipped or shattered with even the slightest blow. Consequently, the task of the parent is to shape the will (1 Tim. 3:4–5) while protecting the spirit (Eph. 6:4). An abundance of proverbs will be our counselors as we equip ourselves for this important battle of disciplining our children.

I. Discipline Should Be Punitive

The Old Testament concept of *discipline* revolves around the Hebrew word *yasar.* The word, along with its derivatives, means "to chastise" or "to discipline." The theological basis for discipline is grounded in the covenant relationship the Lord establishes with His people (cf. Deut. 8:1–5, 16–18).[2] Quoting Proverbs 3:11–12, Hebrews 12:5–6 states that God deals with us "as sons," and further, if we are without discipline, we are "illegitimate children and not sons" (Heb. 12:8). The discipline a father inflicts on his son can be painful. As the writer of Hebrews says, "All discipline for the moment seems not to be joyful, but sorrowful" (v. 11). The term *yasar* is punitive in nature and often connotes a certain harshness by which the correction is made. For example, the *rod,* used nine times in Proverbs, is often connected with the word *discipline:*

> He who spares his rod hates his son,
> But he who loves him disciplines him diligently.
> (Prov. 13:24)
> Foolishness is bound up in the heart of a child;
> The rod of discipline will remove it far from him.
> (22:15)

The rod is not to be used as an end in itself, as a vent for the parent's anger. Rather, its use should be correctional, as a means of guidance

---

1. Dr. James Dobson, *The Strong-Willed Child* (Wheaton, Ill.: Tyndale House Publishers, 1978), p. 36.

2. See *Theological Wordbook of the Old Testament,* ed. R. Laird Harris and Gleason L. Archer, Jr. (Chicago: Moody Press, 1980), pp. 386–87.

into right behavior. Loving parents inflict temporary discomfort on their children by spanking, to spare them the long-range disaster of an unruly life. Consequently, "biblical discipline (chastisement) is goal oriented: it seeks to develop a godly person who is responsive to the Lord and who walks in His ways."[3] As well as being punitive, discipline is also *instructive.*

II. Discipline Should Be Instructive

The second key word in our study is *yakach,* translated "reproof." Often, it is used in conjunction with *discipline:* "My son, do not reject the discipline of the Lord / Or loathe His reproof" (Prov. 3:11). Whereas *discipline* carries with it the notion of physical chastisement, *reproof* is a broader word involving the entire process from punishment to instruction. *Discipline* deals more with correcting the external, overt act of disobedience. *Reproof,* however, deals more with providing inward instruction. Proverbs tells us that wisdom (29:15), honor (13:18), and understanding (15:32) belong to the person who listens to *reproof.* Reproof is the verbal way of reaffirming the standard established in the home and the child's accountability to it. Taken together, the words *discipline* and *reproof* describe that correction as a well-thought-out process where control is balanced with love. Discipline is not a back of the hand given in anger, and reproof is not a brutal tongue-lashing. That type of correction withers the child's self-esteem. That's why Paul advises, "Fathers, do not exasperate your children, that they may not lose heart" (Col. 3:21).

III. Discipline Should Be Properly Motivated

For discipline to have a positive and enduring effect, it must be properly motivated.

A. With love. As truth should be spoken "in love" (Eph. 4:15), discipline and reproof should be done "in love":

For whom the Lord loves He reproves. (Prov. 3:12a)
He who loves [his son] disciplines him diligently. (13:24)

"It is important to remember that no discipline can be effective out of the context of loving relationships and that caring enough to let each child know that he or she is truly important is essential."[4]

B. With delight. One way that love is communicated is the degree of *delight* the parent has in the child:

3. Lawrence O. Richards, *Expository Dictionary of Bible Words* (Grand Rapids, Mich.: Zondervan Publishing House, 1985), p. 228.

4. Richards, *Expository Dictionary,* p. 229.

For whom the Lord loves He reproves,
Even as a father, the son in whom he delights.
(3:12)

This underlying idea of *delight* means "to be pleased with, to accept favorably, to admire" (cf. Prov. 3:12; 11:1, 20; 12:22; 14:35). Affirming your love for the child at some time during the discipline process helps to preserve and enhance the child's sense of self-worth.

Some Personal Application

Do you delight in your children? When is the last time you told them? When is the last time you took your children aside—whether the children are three or thirty-three—and expressed what a delight they are to you? When is the last time, in the midst of discipline or perhaps after, that you tenderly expressed to your children your favor and acceptance? A father and mother who genuinely delight in their children convey that delight in their reproof.

IV. Discipline Should Begin Early

The question of *when* discipline should begin is a subject of considerable debate, but the Scriptures are clear that it should begin early.

A. While it is dawn. In Proverbs 13:24—"He who loves [his son] disciplines him diligently"—the word *diligently* has an interesting background. In its noun form, the word means "dawn." In its adverbial form, it means "at dawn" or "early." Therefore, the word takes on the idea of earnestness or diligence, as often anything done at the crack of dawn is done with earnestness and diligence.

B. While there is hope.

Discipline your son while there is hope,
And do not desire his death. (19:18)
Foolishness is bound up in the heart of a child;
The rod of discipline will remove it far from him.
(22:15)

It is the parents' joint responsibility to remove foolishness from the child during the brief years while the child is under their care. (By foolishness, we don't mean childishness; we mean the behavior of a fool.) This is the time *while there is hope.* In ancient times, if the child became set in his ways of disobedience and rebellion to the extent that the parents could no longer control him, he was to be taken before the elders of the city and stoned (Deut. 21:18–21). This is what is meant by "desire his death." Like snapshots taken from various angles, Proverbs

29

captures the many sides of a fool: "Wickedness is like sport to a fool" (10:23). "The way of a fool is right in his own eyes" (12:15). He is "arrogant and careless" (14:16), "rejects his father's discipline" (15:5), is "perverse in speech" (19:1), quarrelsome (20:3), and "always loses his temper" (29:15). An example of a man who has never had foolishness driven from him is found in Proverbs 19:13:

> The foolishness of a man subverts his way,
> And his heart rages against the Lord.

Spiritual rebellion in an adult can often be traced to a childhood in which foolishness was never decisively dealt with. As he grows older, foolishness wins out over wisdom and takes the steering wheel of his life, "subverting his way" to disastrous consequences. An example of this can be seen in Eli's sons (1 Sam. 3:11–14).[5] A similarly grotesque portrait of a woman who has never had foolishness driven from her is found in Proverbs 14:1:

> The wise woman builds her house,
> But the foolish tears it down with her own hands.

This is a heartbreaking portrait of a young woman who never had the rod applied consistently and correctly. She may approach marriage with stars in her eyes, but soon those stars will turn to sand. Day by day, board by board, relationship by relationship, she tears her home apart—with her own hands.

V. Guidelines for Disciplining Your Child

Depending on the presence or absence of proper discipline, your child will be a delight and a comfort to you (Prov. 29:17) or a source of shame (v. 15). Here are some guidelines which will help you in establishing that discipline in your home:

A. Define the boundaries before they are enforced. This gives the child a sense of clarity about the values in your home.

B. Enforce the boundaries when they are violated. This gives the child a sense of consistency which helps to establish those values permanently.

C. Discipline in private. This protects the child's self-esteem from excessive and needless embarrassment.

D. Discipline with a neutral object, like a rod. The Scripture does not say "hand."

E. Discipline with dignity. Remember, your child is a person too.

F. Be in control of yourself. After all, isn't self-control what you're trying to teach your child?

---

5. See Chuck Swindoll's, "Danger Signals of a Disintegrating Family," *Insights* (Winter 1985), pp. 21–25.

G. Reassure and teach after the confrontation is over.
Here is where the demonstration of love and delight is most important.

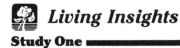 *Living Insights*

God has a twofold approach to discipline: the rod and reproof. Biblical discipline is the *combination* of these two concepts.

• What do the following verses teach you about God's design for discipline? Half of them deal with the rod; the other half deal with reproof. Copy the references in your notebook and next to each, jot down the observations you make concerning discipline.

The Rod	Reproof
Proverbs 10:13	Proverbs 1:23
13:24	1:25
14:3	1:30
22:8	3:11
22:15	5:12
23:13	10:17
23:14	12:1
26:3	13:18
29:15	15:5
	15:10
	15:31
	15:32
	29:1
	29:15

Continued on next page

🌸 Living Insights

For whom the Lord loves He reproves,

Even as a father, the son in whom he delights. (Prov. 3:12)

Reproving is instructing, guiding, and verbally accenting the discipleship aspects of our parenting. Much of reproof is spontaneous as the need arises. But there is another aspect that we can plan into our schedule.

- Do you delight in your children? How? In what ways do you show admiration for each of your children? Write down the names of your children and next to each name, outline a plan of action of how you will show your delight for that child in the next two weeks. It can be anything from a celebration to a more subtle expression of delight. Remember: You cannot expect to make a disciple in the genuine sense if this ingredient of "delight" is missing.

The Ministry of the Rod
1 Samuel 2:11–3:13

"Training up" a child, remember, suggests two things, according to the usage of the Hebrew word. It conveys the idea of taming something that is wild, and also indicates developing a taste for something good and nourishing. When we train our children, we initiate techniques that bring about a submissive will. We also discover ways to develop our children's taste so that they delight in things that are wholesome and right. None of this is naturally known by a child. These are things parents need to instill during those growing-up years in the home. When this is done correctly, God promises that even when our children reach maturity, that indescribable age of independence, they won't turn away from the training they have received. In this lesson, we will be looking at a man who failed to follow these principles—a man named Eli, who failed to tame his sons and develop in them a taste for the ways of God.

I. The Seriousness of Rebellion

Before we look at the life of Eli, we will first examine the seriousness with which God views rebellion, and then consider its effect upon a community and upon society as a whole.

A. In Israel. The Mosaic legislation regarding the moral preservation of Israel, although strict and often severe, helped communicate to God's people how seriously He viewed sin. As you read the passage in Deuteronomy 21, you can't help but flinch. If the parents' rod was not sufficient to curb the rebellion in their child, then God would wield a bigger rod in the hands of the city's elders.

> "If any man has a stubborn and rebellious son who will not obey his father or his mother, and when they chastise him, he will not even listen to them, then his father and mother shall seize him, and bring him out to the elders of his city at the gateway of his home town. And they shall say to the elders of his city, 'This son of ours is stubborn and rebellious, he will not obey us, he is a glutton and a drunkard.' Then all the men of his city shall stone him to death; so you shall remove the evil from your midst, and all Israel shall hear of it and fear." (vv. 18–21)[1]

1. A few notes of observation might serve to clarify these verses. First, the extreme measures were not brought against a young child but an older one—one accused, among other things, of being a *drunkard* (v. 20). Second, community discipline was turned to as a last resort, only after parental discipline had been continually spurned over the years. In verse 20, the adjectives *stubborn* and *rebellious,* modifying *son,* indicate these are character qualities of

Footnote continued on next page

33

This extreme action taken by the leaders of the community is similar to the biological process whereby white blood cells will surround a harmful infection, isolating and attacking it until it is destroyed. The attack is brutal and final—but necessary if the health of the body is to be maintained. Infection will inflame healthy cells and spread throughout the entire body if not decisively dealt with. Similarly, rebellion has a way of stubbornly clinging to the child all through life and infecting all with whom the child comes in contact.[2] Hence, the extreme measures prescribed in Deuteronomy 21.

B. In society. As we turn to the New Testament, we notice that rebellion's fist has been raised in defiance to God since the Fall:

> For since the creation of the world His invisible attributes, His eternal power and divine nature, have been clearly seen, being understood through what has been made, so that they are without excuse. For even though they knew God, they did not honor Him as God, or give thanks; but they became futile in their speculations, and their foolish heart was darkened. (Rom. 1:20–21)

In response to this revolt against the Creator's authority, God opened the floodgates which had restrained the consequences of that rebellion:

> And just as they did not see fit to acknowledge God any longer, God gave them over to a depraved mind, to do those things which are not proper, being filled with all unrighteousness, wickedness, greed, evil; full of envy, murder, strife, deceit, malice; they are gossips, slanderers, haters of God, insolent, arrogant, boastful, inventors of evil, disobedient to parents. (vv. 28–30)

Notice especially the description in verse 30—*disobedient to parents.* This phrase is used again in the New Testament, this time in reference to the end times:

> But realize this, that in the last days difficult times will come. For men will be lovers of self, lovers of money, boastful, arrogant, revilers, disobedient to parents.... (2 Tim. 3:1–2)

the child. Therefore, traits developed over a long period of time are in view and not an isolated act of rebellion. Third, the child's rebellion is so deep-rooted that he cannot be reasoned with—"when they chastise him, *he will not even listen to them*" (v. 18b, emphasis added).

2. This idea of rebellion having a permeating effect within the community is inferred by the words in verse 21, "so you shall remove the evil from your midst" (see also Paul's advice on maintaining the moral purity of the church in 1 Cor. 5:13). The threat of this extreme form of discipline also served as a deterrent—"and all Israel shall hear of it and fear" (v. 21b).

The society which runs rampant is a society that produces children who are disobedient to their parents.

Some Personal Application

From Eden to the end times, the world has been, and will be, in revolt against God. This is the world in which you and I must live and raise our children. If we are not actively helping to mold them into the image of Christ, be assured, they will be molded into the image of the world (see Rom. 12:2). The world's image is reflected in the deeds of the flesh (Gal. 5:19–20). Next to that image, standing tall and radiant, is the image of Christ reflected in the fruit of the Spirit (vv. 22–23). Which image would you want your child to be conformed to? What are you doing to model those qualities so that your child has a clear visual aid to follow?

II. Five Reasons for Rebellion

We will now look at Eli's family and five reasons why his children grew up bent on being disobedient and rebellious. We will begin the study by looking to 1 Samuel 1:3. "And the two sons of Eli, Hophni and Phinehas were priests to the Lord there." At this time in Jewish history (sometime between the fall of Samaria in 722 B.C. and the post-Solomonic era) Eli was the high priest. Following in their father's vocational footsteps, his sons entered the priesthood also. However, several things distinguished their steps from the steps of their father.

A. Not knowing the Lord. Like shoes without feet, Hophni and Phinehas were missing something vital to fill them and give them life—they were missing a relationship with the Lord. It should have been a prerequisite for their priesthood, but perhaps Eli, as a compromising parent, soft-pedaled their applications.

Now the sons of Eli were worthless men;[3] they did not know the Lord. (1 Sam. 2:12)

---

3. *Worthless men* literally means "sons of Belial" and is rendered such in the Authorized, or King James Version, while the Revised Standard Version has *base fellows* and the New English Bible has *scoundrels*. The term *Belial* usually occurs in such expressions as "sons of Belial" (Deut. 13:13) or "daughter of Belial" (1 Sam. 1:16), translated in the New American Standard Bible, *worthless men* and *worthless woman*, respectively. In Jewish apocalyptic literature, *Belial* is used to describe Satan or the Antichrist. Paul uses the word in this sense in 2 Corinthians 6:15. *Belial* comes from two Hebrew words meaning "without" and "profit." In Proverbs the *worthless man* is equated with the *wicked man* whose life is characterized by lying (6:12) and digging up evil (16:27).

It is evident from the passages describing Eli's ministry that he was a man of integrity, dedicated to the Lord (cf. 1:9–18, 2:18–21). But apparently he was too busy with the demands of his ministry at *the house of God* to be involved in any significant way during his sons' formative years.[4] Consequently, since the cost of commitment wasn't paid during their childhood years, the bills all came due in their adulthood. The first entry in the ledger is seen in 1 Samuel 2:12–14:

> Now the sons of Eli were worthless men; they did not know the Lord and the custom of the priests with the people. When any man was offering a sacrifice, the priest's servant would come while the meat was boiling, with a three-pronged fork in his hand. Then he would thrust it into the pan, or kettle, or caldron, or pot; all that the fork brought up the priest would take for himself. Thus they did in Shiloh to all the Israelites who came there.

The priests who served in the house of God lived off the offerings that were brought there by the people. However, the priests could not pick and choose the best meat for themselves, and they couldn't go back for seconds. Instead, there was a certain established custom, described in verses 13–14, which determined how much meat the priests received and how much was left as an offering to the Lord. But Hophni and Phinehas weren't used to restraints, as the lengthening of the accounts payable column in verses 15–17 indicates:

> Also, before they burned the fat, the priest's servant would come and say to the man who was sacrificing, "Give the priest meat for roasting, as he will not take boiled meat from you, only raw." And if the man said to him, "They must surely burn the fat first, and then take as much as you desire," then he would say, "No, but you shall give it to me now; and if not, I will take it by force."[5] Thus the sin of the young men was very great before the Lord, for the men despised the offering of the Lord.

It is obvious from the passage that Eli's sons wanted *immediate* gratification of their desires—"give it to me now" (v. 16b).

---

4. The New Testament has some very specific principles about the relationship between parental responsibilities at home and ministerial responsibilities at church (cf. 1 Tim. 3:4–5, 12). Essentially, if a person cannot manage "his own household," that sphere of responsibility shouldn't be enlarged to include the household of God.

5. The burning of the fat as an offering to the Lord is established in the levitical code for priests in Leviticus 3:3–5. Obviously, Eli's sons not only had little regard for traditional customs but for Scripture as well (compare Lev. 3:16 with 1 Sam. 2:12b–13).

Furthermore, they would allow nothing to stand in the way of those desires being met—"and if not, I will take it by force" (v. 16c).

B. Tolerating fleshly sin. We see that with no discipline leveed against them, their surging passion to satisfy the flesh breaks the banks and spills over into sexual gratification:

> Now Eli was very old; and he heard all that his sons were doing to all Israel, and how they lay with the women who served at the doorway of the tent of meeting. (v. 22)

They not only committed immorality; they did it with a brazen and blasphemous arrogance (v. 22b).

C. Failing to apply correct discipline. Aware of his sons' disobedience, Eli makes only an anemic attempt at discipline:

> And he said to them, "Why do you do such things, the evil things that I hear from all these people? No, my sons; for the report is not good which I hear the Lord's people circulating. If one man sins against another, God will mediate for him; but if a man sins against the Lord, who can intercede for him?" (vv. 23–25a)

D. Failing to teach respect for authority. At the heart of their rebellion was the fact that Hophni and Phinehas had no respect for authority. This can be seen in the last half of verse 25: "But they would not listen to the voice of their father."

E. Failing to develop a spirit of submissiveness. Since Eli refused to take a firm stand with his sons, tolerating their evil, we see God taking over their books, declaring them bankrupt, and calling in all their outstanding debts:

> "Behold, I am about to do a thing in Israel at which both ears of everyone who hears it will tingle. In that day I will carry out against Eli all that I have spoken concerning his house, from beginning to end. For I have told him that I am about to judge his house forever for the iniquity which he knew, because his sons brought a curse on themselves and he did not rebuke them." (3:11–13)

The failure of Eli is seen in verse 13: "He did not rebuke them." The Hebrew word translated *rebuke* has the root meaning "to grow dim" or "to be weak." In this form it means "to cause to grow dim" or "to weaken." Eli did nothing to dim the fiery passions that burned out of control in his sons. He did nothing to weaken their rebellious wills which stood hard and fast against God. In essence, he did nothing to help develop a submissive spirit in them.

Living Insights

Study One ━━━

First Samuel 1–3 contains the record of an ironic tragedy. Eli, the priest, had godless sons. The man put on earth to be God's representative dropped the ball in the most crucial arena—his home.

- We can learn valuable lessons from the mistakes of others. None of us as parents want our children to disobey. Read over the first three chapters of 1 Samuel once again. Then, locate another version of the Scriptures and read the same passage carefully. Seeing verses in a fresh translation or paraphrase can help us gain new insights into God's Word.

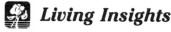 ## Living Insights

Study Two ━━━

One of the more curious aspects of child-raising is the correlation between how you discipline your children and how you were disciplined by your parents. Samuel saw the mistakes made by Eli, yet imitated many of them himself. Use the following list to help you analyze this fascinating phenomenon.

- Describe the parenting style of your parents in one sentence.
- Describe your parenting style in one sentence.
- What are you repeating in your style that you saw in your parents?
- What are you doing that is different from what your parents did?
- What's the best thing your parents taught you?
- What would you most like to teach your children?

Training Your Child
Deuteronomy 6:4–9

How-to books seem to crowd bookstores like schoolboys lining up for recess. Pushing and shoving to line the shelves, they elbow their way into the marketplace, promising to teach us everything from how to lose weight to how to gain a fortune in real estate. Regarding books on training children, everyone from housewives to Harvard psychologists seem to have something in print. In this lesson, we want to check out a classic from an ancient library in Jewish history. It's a thin little volume, only six verses long, found on a bottom shelf in Deuteronomy.

I. God's Classic Volume for Training Children
The passage for our study is Deuteronomy 6:4–9, known to the Jews as the *Shema:*[1]

> "Hear, O Israel! The Lord is our God, the Lord is one! And you shall love the Lord your God with all your heart and with all your soul and with all your might. And these words, which I am commanding you today, shall be on your heart; and you shall teach them diligently to your sons and shall talk of them when you sit in your house and when you walk by the way and when you lie down and when you rise up. And you shall bind them as a sign on your hand and they shall be as frontals on your forehead. And you shall write them on the doorposts of your house and on your gates."

Deuteronomy was given to the Israelites when they were emerging from the wilderness and standing on the edge of the land of milk and honey—the Promised Land. However, there were some things about the new land that weren't so promising. Dwelling in the land were the godless and immoral Canaanites. God gave Israel a mandate to possess the land by defeating and driving out the Canaanites. In no way were the Israelites to cohabit with them, adopt their gods, or embrace their lifestyle (Deut. 7:1–5).[2]

---

1. *Shema* is from the Hebrew word translated "hear" in verse 4. To this day, Orthodox Jews recite the *Shema* daily, along with Deuteronomy 11:13–21 and Numbers 15:37–41. In Mark 12:29–30, Jesus cites Deuteronomy 6:4–5 as the foremost commandment.

2. "Tablets recovered from Ugarit afford a full description of the Canaanite pantheon, and they throw startling new light on the degrading, orgiastic nature of Canaanite fertility-worship.... Ugaritic texts make it evident that Canaanite religion was of an intensely corrupt and immoral kind, which pervaded and even contaminated other Near Eastern religions and thoroughly merited the divine commands relating to the destruction of the devotees of Canaanite religion (Gen. 15:16, Exod. 23–24 et al.)" (*Dictionary of Biblical Archaeology*, ed. Edward M. Blaiklock and R. K. Harrison [Grand Rapids, Mich.: Regency Reference Library, Zondervan Publishing House, 1983], pp. 117–18).

II. Training Must Begin in the Parents' Lives

Before God reveals His wisdom on training children, He reveals Himself and draws the parents to Him.

A. Their faith in God.

"Hear, O Israel! The Lord is our God, the Lord is one!"[3]
(v. 4)

The statement is a simple confession of faith. Unlike the many Canaanite gods who were unpredictable and seldom lived in any kind of harmony, the Lord God of Israel is *one*—a unity, both unique and ultimate. The Canaanites were always shifting allegiances from one deity to another; the Israelites dealt with only one God. And as the Canaanites were never quite sure whether their loyalty to one god would protect them or inflame the wrath of another, the Israelites could depend on the fact that the Lord was *their* God and that He dealt with them on the basis of a consistent, righteous standard.

B. Their allegiance to God.
With the monumental task before Israel of driving out the godless culture of the Canaanites, no less than total loyalty was required of them by God:

"And you shall love the Lord your God with all your
heart and with all your soul and with all your might."
(v. 5)

Some Probing Questions

Love is the heart and soul and might of our relationship with God. Without it, whatever instruction we give our children is like a noisy gong. And the longer and louder we clang our cymbals, the more our children will just cover their ears. How vital is your relationship with the Lord? Is it *with all your heart*—or is it hollow? Is it *with all your soul*—or is it superficial? Is it *with all your might*—or is it a half-hearted attempt?

III. God Commands the Parents to Train Their Children

Deuteronomy 6:4–5 establishes the basis for effective parenting: knowing and loving the Lord. And if we love the Lord with all of our heart, then *His* words will be on our heart:

"And these words, which I am commanding you today,
shall be on your heart." (v. 6; cf. Luke 6:45)

---

3. The Hebrew word for "one" is *echad* and may suggest a unity of persons within the Godhead. The same word is found in Genesis 2:24 where *one* is used of the union between Adam and Eve.

It is out of the overflow of a vital, loving relationship with God that parents are to instruct their children. The teaching should be conducted diligently, continually, and with a view to preparing the child for life.

A. **Diligently.** In the first part of verse 7—"and you shall teach them diligently to your sons"—the words *teach diligently* are a translation of the Hebrew word *shanan,* meaning "to sharpen."[4] It is a vivid word conveying the idea that the teaching is purposed to give your child a sharp edge for living—keen, perceptive, and discerning.

B. **Continually.** The parents' relationship with the Lord and their relay of His truth serve to *sharpen* the child's character. And so the edge doesn't get dull, the teaching is to be *continual:*

> "And [you] shall talk of them when you sit in your
> house and when you walk by the way and when you
> lie down and when you rise up." (v. 7)

Moral and biblical education is best accomplished not in Sunday school or in seminars but at home. It is most effective not in a formal setting but in a casual one—sitting around the dinner table, taking a walk in the park, tucking the children in bed, taking them to school.

C. **To prepare the child for life.** The training you give your children should prepare them for the real world as "children of God above reproach in the midst of a crooked and perverse generation" (Phil. 2:15). In order for the Israelites to prepare their children for the real world of Canaan, they needed to keep God's commands firmly in hand and in the forefront of their minds:

> "And you shall bind them as a sign on your hand and
> they shall be as frontals on your forehead." (Deut. 6:8)

The Pharisees in Jesus' day took this passage literally and wore small leather boxes called phylacteries, which contained the *Shema* along with Deuteronomy 11:13–21 and Exodus 13:1–16 written on parchment. At the time of morning prayer (except on the Sabbath and festival days), every Jewish male over thirteen would bind the phylacteries with leather straps around their forehead and left forearm. In Matthew 23:5, Jesus speaks condemningly of this ostentatious show. The command in Deuteronomy 6:8 should rather be seen in a figurative sense, similar to Proverbs 7:3, where Solomon instructs his son to treasure his commandments, to "bind them on your fingers;/

---

4. The verb is used of sharpening swords and arrows in Deuteronomy 32:41; Isaiah 5:28; Psalm 45:5, 120:4; Proverbs 25:18.

Write them on the tablet of your heart." Finally, verse 9 of Deuteronomy 6 suggests movement away from home:

"And you shall write them on the doorposts of your house and on your gates."

Again, the Jews interpreted this in a literal sense and placed those same passages into small containers and attached them to their doorposts. But the picture is really one of progression outside of the home. Through this imagery God appears to be saying that the children are leaving, preparing for departure out into the world, and that every step of the way these commandments are to be reminders to them. Consequently, the Jews were not to tuck the verses away in storage containers like time capsules. Rather, they were to treasure them in their hearts because love for the Lord was never meant to be external and lifeless but internal and vital. May that love pump through *your* heart and through every artery and capillary of your existence.

🌺 Living Insights

Study One

We're in the midst of studying a classic portion of God's Word. Deuteronomy 6:4–9 is a foundational text on training children. Is this passage a part of your working capital as you attempt to be a godly parent?

● The most effective way to take these truths with you in your parenting is to memorize them. If six verses are more than you feel you can handle all at once, select two or three that will be most helpful to you. Write out the words on index cards and begin by reading them aloud over and over. As you continue this process, you'll soon be reading less and memorizing more.

Living Insights

Nighttime can reduce things down to the basics. Dad comes home late from the office. His son is fast asleep, yet Dad bends over and kisses him. Filled with love for his boy, Dad pulls a tablet from his briefcase and writes his son a letter. In the letter, he reinforces his love, commitment, and admiration for his fine young boy. If you look closely, you can see a tear in this dad's eye as he finishes the note and places it by the boy's bed.

- Mom and Dad, write a letter to your child. Make it personal. Use it as a vehicle to communicate positive thoughts to each of your children. Be open, honest, and vulnerable. And don't forget, as you write this note, it's OK to have a tear in your eye.

The Home Training of Jesus
Luke 2, Hebrews 5:8

It seems the older we get as parents, the more dear our memories become. Nostalgia frames each of the photographs buried in our family albums. If you're like most parents, you probably treasure those early photos of your children the most. And like most parents, probably wish you had taken more pictures during that time. So far in our studies, we've mainly looked at our own family albums. We've been studying principles in order that we might fill those pages with photographs that are vibrant, colorful, and in sharp focus with God's Word. In this study, however, we're going to browse through a family album on the coffee table of Mary and Joseph, the parents of the only perfect child—Jesus.

I. From Infancy to Twelve Years of Age

The album we have of Jesus as a boy contains only two photographs: one of His childhood (Luke 2:39–40); the other as He stands on the threshold of His teenage years (Luke 2:41–52). Neither are fully developed, but enough of the lines are present to give resolution to those early, formative years. If you pick up the first snapshot and squint a little, you'll see some illuminating principles in the shadows:

> And when they had performed everything according to
> the Law of the Lord, they returned to Galilee, to their
> own city of Nazareth. And the Child continued to grow
> and become strong, increasing in wisdom; and the grace
> of God was upon Him. (Luke 2:39–40)

In verse 39 we see Mary and Joseph during those early years of Jesus' infancy. Pictured here are two *committed* parents—committed to the Lord and committed to their child. And their commitment is meticulous, "[performing] *everything* according to the Law of the Lord" (emphasis added).

A. Physical growth. Verse 40 turns our focus onto Jesus. The first detail that catches our attention is His physical stature: "And the Child continued to grow and become strong." The casualness of the statement, "the Child continued to grow," could suggest there was no force there. No parental push. You don't get the impression Mary and Joseph were anxious about preparing Jesus for His debut into society. Obviously, He was a uniquely gifted young man; yet He was allowed to grow at His own pace. Written between the lines is a normal process of calm, consistent, unhurried development.

B. Mental growth. Just as Jesus continued to grow physically, He developed mentally and emotionally as well, *increasing in wisdom*. Literally, the phrase means "He continued to be filled with wisdom." The Greek tense conveying *continued action* and the idea of *being filled up* together suggest a process. Paul, writing from prison, describes how this process worked in Timothy's life. First, he mentions in 2 Timothy 3:13 the conditions of the world in which they lived: "evil men and impostors will proceed from bad to worse, deceiving and being deceived." In verses 14–15, he exhorts Timothy to be on the alert by continuing to follow the step-by-step process which began in his home:

> You, however, continue in the things you have learned and become convinced of, knowing from whom you have learned them; and that from childhood you have known the sacred writings which are able to give you the wisdom that leads to salvation through faith which is in Christ Jesus.

The first thing we observe is *the importance of childhood training.* In 2 Timothy 1:5, the door to Timothy's home stands ajar, and we are given a peek at his childhood influences. "I am mindful of the sincere faith within you, which first dwelt in your grandmother Lois, and your mother Eunice." What a heritage! His grandmother was a godly woman, his mother was a godly woman, and both passed on the same traits to Timothy. In the relay of truth in Timothy's line, no one dropped the baton, thus preparing the young man for living in an ungodly world. Another observation is from 2 Timothy 3:14–15: *childhood training is a process.* Timothy's first tottering step was receiving *knowledge* regarding *the sacred writings.* Verses 16–17 delineate just how applicable these writings are. The second, firmer step in the process was *learning* or appropriating the knowledge imparted to him. The confident third step was the development of *personal conviction.* Finally, he learned to walk in *wisdom:* "from childhood you have known the sacred writings which are able to give you the wisdom ..." (v. 15). Wisdom is the skill of applying biblical principles to everyday life. Essentially, it is looking at life from God's point of view.

C. Spiritual growth. According to Luke 2:40, as Jesus increased in stature and in wisdom, "the grace of God was upon Him." As His life began to unfold, grace descended upon Him like dew upon a morning flower. Spiritual life seems to have a delicate timing mechanism ticking away in the seeds of our children's souls. In its own season—when the ground is fertile—germination will take place. And when the angle of the sun is right, the grace of God will bring that bud to full flower. It doesn't take a parent's pulling on the petals or fertilizing it to death. Growth is a process both in the physical realm and in the spiritual (see

Mark 4:26–28). We can plant seeds and water, but ultimately, it is God that causes the growth (1 Cor. 3:6).

II. From Adolescence to Thirty Years of Age

Turning from Jesus' childhood years, we see Him as a young man in Luke 2:51–52. Aside from the incident in the temple (vv. 41–50), we know nothing more of His early years.

A. His subjection to His parents. As we stare at this photo of Mary, Joseph, and Jesus all returning from Jerusalem, something incongruous catches our eye:

> And He went down with them, and came to Nazareth;
> and He continued in subjection to them; and His
> mother treasured all these things in her heart. (v. 51)

Our eyes hesitate over the word *subjection.* The Greek word is a military term which means "to fall in rank under the authority of another." Understanding that, let's look again at the picture. To one side of the photograph we see Mary and Joseph walking on the road to Nazareth. Walking with them and in *subjection* to them is the young Jesus. The juxtaposition highlights the contrast: Perfect child—imperfect parents. Creator—creatures. King of Kings—subjects of the King. Yet, in spite of the apparent miscasting, He submits to their authority. And suddenly the picture becomes breathtakingly beautiful.

B. His development. The last verse in Luke 2 reads: "And Jesus kept increasing in wisdom and stature, and in favor with God and men." The picture resembles the one in verse 40, but if you compare the two closely, you will find that wisdom and physical development have changed places. *Wisdom* is in the foreground overshadowing *stature.* The Greek word translated *increasing* indicates more vigorous movement and adds another dimension to the picture. Jesus, as a teenager, continued to progress physically, but His wisdom was vigorously outdistancing His physical development. The final description regarding His development, "in favor with God and men," pictures Jesus as balanced. Both His vertical and His horizontal relationships were in harmony and in balance.

An Underdeveloped Negative

As we close the album, we see the words from Hebrews 5:8 engraved in gold lettering on the cover: "Although He was a Son, He learned obedience from the things which He suffered." The pictures we have seen thus far show a growing boy living out His childhood in favor with God and men. However, the pictures to be developed later in Jesus' life were ones of persecution, betrayal, trials, and

---

crucifixion—of pain and suffering. Most parents seem intent on sparing their children from all forms of suffering. They intercede or intervene whenever pain threatens to touch their child. This protectiveness is natural but should be held in balance with the reality that most of the important lessons of life are learned through pain and suffering (cf. Lam. 3:27).

Living Insights

Study One

The early years of Christ's life break down into three distinct areas: spiritual, mental/emotional, and physical. The key to maturity is growth in all of these areas. Let's correlate these facets of life with a familiar passage from God's Word.

- Galatians 5:22–23 contain nine traits of the Christian life that we commonly call the fruit of the Spirit. These characteristics have obvious effects on our spiritual life, but do they affect our mental/emotional and physical aspects as well? Spend a few minutes thinking through this issue. The following chart can be used to guide your thinking.

The Fruit of the Spirit in Every Aspect of My Life			
Fruit of the Spirit	How Does This Affect Me Spiritually?	How Does This Affect Me Mentally / Emotionally?	How Does This Affect Me Physically?
Love			
Joy			
Peace			
Patience			
Kindness			
Goodness			
Faithfulness			
Gentleness			
Self-control			

Continued on next page

🐝 *Living Insights*

An important portion of this study was spotlighting the children's obedience in our homes. There are some questions we can ask in order to help determine if children are in submission to their parents. Try these four questions on your own children! A good discussion ought to result, perhaps around the dinner table or in the family room.

- Do you cooperate with your parents' desires without griping?
- Do you happily give up your rights when there is a conflict in the schedule at home?
- Do you respond to your parents' counsel and correction with appreciation?
- Do you fulfill your responsibilities thoroughly, regularly, and with a good attitude?

Releasing Your Child

Selected Scripture

Picture yourself at an archery tournament in which the value of your whole life is at stake. The time to take your shot at the target arrives. Engaging the feathered end of the arrow securely to the taut string, you take a cursory look toward what now seems to be a too-distant target. You inhale, hold a second, then exhale with uncertainty. You lift the bow into position. Imperceptible beads of sweat pincushion your forehead's hairline. With hesitation, you pull back the bowstring. You squint down the shaft of the arrow toward the target. The beads on your forehead string together loosely to form broken necklaces of sweat. Suddenly, your eye catches a bent in the arrow, further undermining your confidence. OK—exhale—relax. Put down the bow and let's talk this thing out. Releasing an arrow under such circumstances can be a tense, shaky experience. Releasing children into the world can be an experience of equal anxiety. In one sense, it is natural for this period of release to be difficult. In another sense, we make it difficult for ourselves. Hopefully, this lesson will mop a little of the sweat from your brow as that moment approaches.

I. Why Releasing Your Child Comes Hard

Releasing offspring is the natural order of both plant and animal worlds. As inevitably as dandelion seeds parachute off to new soil and as instinctively as young birds stretch new wings to leave their nests, so God has designed children to grow up and start new homes of their own:

> For this cause a man shall leave his father and his mother,
> and shall cleave to his wife; and they shall become one
> flesh. (Gen. 2:24)

In spite of how natural, how inevitable, how instinctive, and how scriptural it may be, releasing children is still difficult for most parents.

A. Sometimes, parents build themselves into their children.
The first reason for difficulty in releasing children is when parents build *themselves* into their children rather than developing the children according to how *God* designed them. Fathers and mothers alike are sometimes guilty of reliving their lives through their children. Often their motives are good—an "if-I-had-it-all-to-do-over-again" approach. So they try to fill up in their children's lives what was lacking in *their* own childhood experience. In doing so, a measure of their identity and their dreams is passed on to the children. Consequently, when they leave, a part of the parent leaves with them. And the withdrawal pains can be excruciating.

49

B. Sometimes, the parental relationship overshadows the marital relationship. The second cause for difficulty in releasing children is revealed in Ephesians 5:22–33. In this text God discusses the home with husbands and wives.

> Wives, be subject to your own husbands. . . . (v. 22)
> Husbands, love your wives. . . . (v. 25)
> Husbands ought also to love their own wives as their own bodies. . . . (v. 28)
> Nevertheless let each individual among you also love his own wife even as himself; and let the wife see to it that she respect her husband. (v. 33)

Children are not mentioned here, because *children were never designed to be the weld that holds the home together.* This explains the second reason parents often find great difficulty in releasing their children: the parental relationship has become stronger than the marriage relationship. The children have been placed in a role they were never designed to fit. Thus, when it's time for the release, it becomes evident that the parents have used their children as the glue to keep their marriage together.

A Curious Observation

It is interesting that the national divorce rate resembles a U-shaped graph. Broken marriages hit a high peak in the early years when the relationship goes through a period of adjustment. When children come, divorce tapers off. Feelings of responsibility and guilt muster enough of a commitment to keep the marriage together. During this time the glue frequently sets as hard as cold concrete. Then, about the time the children leave home, the divorce rate skyrockets off the graph. For those couples who manage to stay together, something else often happens. Insecure parents, who gathered emotional strength from their children that they should have found in their mate, cannot cope with the release. The parents feel they are losing the single thread that tied them to happiness, and that separation from their children becomes a cause for mourning. Husbands and wives, are you establishing a relationship that revolves around your children or around each other? If centered on your children, time will disintegrate that core, and your marriage will collapse in on itself in the vacuum of their absence.

C. Sometimes, parents possess a consuming need for their children. The third reason for a difficult release is unveiled in 2 Corinthians 12:14 where Paul is writing to the church and announces his plans to visit them:

> Here for this third time I am ready to come to you, and I will not be a burden to you; for I do not seek what is yours, but you; for children are not responsible to save up for their parents, but parents for their children.

In a tactful way Paul is saying that he is not coming for money but for them. The principle here is that children do not serve the parents, but parents serve the children. The application we can make is that people do not have children because they *need* them but because they *want* them. Releasing children will be more traumatic for parents who possess an abnormal, unhealthy *need* for them, as opposed to a healthy and unselfish relationship.

II. How to Prepare for Releasing Your Child

Assuming you have a relationship with your children such that you don't try to live your life out through them; assuming you have a relationship with your spouse that is stronger than with the children; assuming you are raising your children not because you need them but because they need you, letting go may still be difficult—*but not devastating.* Turning now from the problems to the solutions, how should we prepare for the time of release?

A. Children should be trained to handle their parents' legacy. Ecclesiastes 2:18–20 contains the embittered words of a man looking at life from a strictly earthly point of view:

> Thus I hated all the fruit of my labor for which I had labored under the sun, for I must leave it to the man who will come after me. And who knows whether he will be a wise man or a fool? Yet he will have control over all the fruit of my labor for which I have labored by acting wisely under the sun. This too is vanity. Therefore I completely despaired of all the fruit of my labor for which I had labored under the sun.

The father described in this passage has labored in his enterprise—lived with it, hammered away at it, fine-tuned it. Tension and pressure made it touch-and-go at times, but he paid the price, made the sacrifices, taxied it down the runway. Finally, he gets it off the ground. At last, the business is airborne and flying high. But sooner or later—his blood pressure's up or his chest pains begin to worsen—father has to bail out. He turns to his co-pilot son who's been allowed to sightsee but never has been taught to fly. With naive eagerness and a sense of newfound power, the son grabs the controls and says, "So long, Dad." Before the joyride has barely gotten underway, the business goes into a tailspin, and then—CRASH!

> ### Conclusions of the Investigation
>
> The team sent to investigate the wreckage unanimously concludes it was caused by pilot error. The son had never learned the lessons the father had, because he had never labored the way the father had. He had never learned the disciplines involved in getting a business off the ground and keeping it in the air. Looking mournfully at the crash site, the investigators mumble to themselves some belated wisdom from the Scriptures. Under the breath of one we hear:
>
> > "If you have run with footmen and they have
> > tired you out,
> > Then how can you compete with the horses?
> > If you fall down in a land of peace,
> > How will you do in the thicket of the Jordan?"
> > (Jer. 12:5)
>
> If your children can't cut it at home in such things as cleaning up their rooms, making their beds, and carrying out other responsibilities, what on earth will they do when they face the *horses* of a competitive career or the *thicket* of marital adjustments? Another investigator shakes his head and mutters as he walks away:
>
> > It is good for a man that he should bear
> > The yoke in his youth. (Lam. 3:27)
>
> Labor, sacrifice, and responsibility are healthy yokes for a person to shoulder during the growing-up years. They will stretch and strengthen the child in preparation for the years to come. Are you preparing your children for the yoke of adult life—or are you pampering them?

B. Keep communicating with your children after they leave. Releasing your child does not mean unlisting your phone number. And "leaving father and mother" does not mean for children to leave them out of their lives. Proverbs 23:22 strikes an encouraging balance:

> Listen to your father who begot you,
> And do not despise your mother when she is old.

But a word of caution is in order for the parents. Once your children leave the nest, your relationship with them changes. Temper your words accordingly.

**C. Look upon release as a process rather than a sudden
event.** Begin the process of letting go the day your child is
born. Anticipate it. Plan for it. Psalm 144:12 somewhat captures
the idea of this process of preparation:

> Let our sons in their youth be as grown-up plants,
> And our daughters as corner pillars fashioned as for
> a palace.

This is a picture of careful nurturing and skillful planning with
regard to the process of raising children. A by-product of preparing children for the seasons and weight of adult life is that
the parents themselves become prepared for their release in the
process.

D. Commit yourself to pray for your children. Prayer
cushions the jolt of release. And, it alleviates a lot of anxiety
(see Job 1:1–5). When you commit yourself to a ministry of
continued prayer for your children, you kneel beside the Lord
Jesus who intercedes for us faithfully from afar (Rom. 8:34). So,
while they're at home, sharpen and straighten the arrows; when
you finally release them—pray they're on target and that they
don't fall short of the glory of God.

┌─ *A Thought to Consider* ─────────────────────
You are the bows from which your children as living
arrows are sent forth.

The archer sees the mark upon the path of the infinite,
and He bends you with His might that His arrows may go
swift and far.

Let your bending in the archer's hand be for gladness;

For even as He loves the arrow that flies, so He loves
also the bow that is stable.[1]

Continued on next page

---

1. Kahlil Gibran, *The Prophet* (New York: Alfred A. Knopf, Inc., 1982), p. 18.

Living Insights

There isn't one particular text of Scripture that addresses releasing your child. So, we've put together a list of various verses that touch on this all-important subject.

- Make a copy of the following chart in your notebook. As you look up the passages, make some general observations first and then zero in on some specific thoughts on how these verses speak to the issue of releasing your child.

Releasing Your Child		
References	General Observations	Specific Thoughts on Releasing Children
Genesis 1:27–28		
2:24		
Ephesians 5:22–33		
2 Corinthians 12:14–15		
Ecclesiastes 2:18–22		
Lamentations 3:27		
Proverbs 23:22		
Psalm 144:12		

Living Insights

Releasing your child is a process. How are you coming along in this area? Let's continue our pattern of personalizing each lesson.

- Take an entire page in your notebook and fill it with your thoughts on releasing your child. If the actual event is still in the future, write about how you're preparing for it now. If your child has already left home, write about how it went . . . the bad and the good. You may be right in the midst of it as you read these words. Has this study been helpful? Why?

Releasing My Child
My Personal Summary

You and Your Daughter
(Part One)
Selected Proverbs

Gone with the Wind, Margaret Mitchell's first and only novel, stands a classic, both as a book and as an adaptation into a film. The backdrop to the story is the war-torn South. But it's not a book about the Civil War. It's a book about one woman—Scarlett O'Hara—a ravishing woman whom men hovered over like flies around a watermelon. But under the coy twirl of the parasol which shaded her fine-china skin, beneath her honeyed, rose-petal lips, behind the flirtatious flutter of her inviting eyes, there hid a woman whose heart was "snares and nets." A conniving, manipulative, even ruthless woman. To bring these characteristics into sharp relief, the author continually places Scarlett beside the kind, pure, accepting Melanie. Next to Melanie, Scarlett pales by comparison, and we see her for what she really is. In similar style, Proverbs often compares and contrasts its characters. In this lesson, we will frame some of those characters that stand side-by-side in the text—the wise woman and the fool; the gracious woman and the contentious.

I. Wise Woman or Foolish

Consider the two women in Proverbs 14:1:

> The wise woman builds her house,
> But the foolish tears it down with her own hands.

Literally, the Hebrew word for *foolish* means "dull, thick, sluggish."[1] The foolish woman of this verse is dulled to wisdom, calloused to correction, and sluggish in her response to God. The result is that destruction lies in the wake of every wave she makes. The term *tears down* comes from a single Hebrew word meaning "to overthrow, to destroy." Board by board, conversation by conversation, circumstance by circumstance, relationship by relationship, she dismantles her house. Her guilt is further underscored by the emphatic phrase *with her own hands.* In the end, as a result of years of troubling her own house, she will only "inherit wind" (cf. 11:29a). No parents want their daughter's life to turn out like that. However, what most parents don't realize is that the foolish woman of Proverbs 14 started out as a foolish *daughter*—a daughter whose foolishness was never fully recognized or effectively dealt with. Here are some diagnostic X rays of a foolish woman which might help you catch the malignancy, if it exists in your daughter, before it proves terminal:

---

1. A portrait of a fool can be found in the study guide titled *Living on the Ragged Edge,* ed. Bill Watkins, from the Bible-teaching ministry of Charles R. Swindoll (Fullerton, Calif.: Insight for Living, 1985), pp. 104–9. See also Derek Kidner's *Proverbs,* Tyndale Old Testament Commentaries, gen. ed., D. J. Wiseman (Downers Grove, Ill.: InterVarsity Press, 1964), pp. 39–41.

A. She is boisterous. Proverbs 9:13 reveals the first clue:

> The woman of folly is boisterous,
> She is naive, and knows nothing.

By *boisterous,* the text doesn't mean energetic or excitable. Rather, the thought is one of commotion and turbulence.[2] Picture an egg beater suddenly lifted out of a mixing bowl and whirling batter all over the kitchen, and you get something of the idea.

B. She makes a mockery of sin. Proverbs 14:9a states: "Fools mock at sin." The foolish woman of Proverbs 9 illustrates this in her making light of adultery:

> "Stolen water is sweet;
> And bread eaten in secret is pleasant." (v. 17)

Her seared conscience is insensitive to sin, causing her to take the passing pleasures of sin lightly, even flippantly. Right and wrong are not important to her; only what is *sweet* and *pleasant.* Her focus on a live-for-the-moment lifestyle is short-sighted and blurs her eyes to the long-term effects of her actions—thus validating that she is truly *naive, and knows nothing.*

C. She is deceptive. Proverbs 14:8b shows us that "the folly of fools is deceit." She can look you eyeball to eyeball and, without batting a lash, deceive you in the most convincing way.

D. She is quarrelsome. A final clue appears in Proverbs 20:3:

> Keeping away from strife is an honor for a man,
> But any fool will quarrel.

The Hebrew term translated *quarrel* means "to burst forth in a rage, a tantrum." A foolish daughter is argumentative and given to rage.

Some Personal Application

Put your daughter behind the X-ray machine for a moment. Now take a good, hard look at the X ray. What do you see? Is she in a constant state of turbulence, filled with uneasiness and commotion? Does she treat sin lightly and flippantly? Is she deceptive and given to frequent lying? More often than not, is she quarrelsome and argumentative? If you see these symptoms in your daughter now, the prognosis for her future is not good. In fact, we may say with a surgeon's frankness, her future holds only heartache and

---

2. "This root, used thirty-four times, means 'cry out,' 'make a loud noise,' or 'be turbulent.' It is a strong word, emphasizing unrest, commotion, strong feeling, or noise" (*Theological Wordbook of the Old Testament,* ed. R. Laird Harris, Gleason L. Archer, Jr., and Bruce K. Waltke [Chicago: Moody Press, 1980], p. 219).

tragedy. If you are the parent of a foolish child, your future is no brighter:

> He who begets a fool does so to his sorrow,
> And the father of a fool has no joy. (Prov. 17:21)

Furthermore, you will be raising a Scarlett whose house will be troubled, torn down, and literally gone with the wind. But if you catch the foolishness early enough, and confront it with the combination of a physician's decisiveness, firmness, and tenderness, then you can grace the world with a Melanie—a wise woman who "builds her house."

II. Contentious Woman or Gracious

Proverbs paints such a fluorescently vivid picture of a contentious woman, it almost glows in the dark!

> And the contentions of a wife are a constant dripping. (19:13b)
> It is better to live in a corner of a roof,
> Than in a house shared with a contentious woman.
> It is better to live in a desert land,
> Than with a contentious and vexing woman. (21:9, 19)
> A constant dripping on a day of steady rain
> And a contentious woman are alike;
> He who would restrain her restrains the wind,
> And grasps oil with his right hand. (27:15–16)

What do you see glowing in the picture? *A leaky faucet.* If you've ever had one keep you awake at night, then you get the picture. *A corner of a roof.* If you've ever been on your roof to fix an antenna, you know things would have to be pretty bad to consider living there permanently. *A desert land.* Blistering, relentless sun. *A constant dripping on a day of steady rain.* Nag, nag, nag, nag, nag—even sounds like dripping rain, doesn't it? *Grasping oil.* Try it sometime; it will drive you crazy. The picture here is of a woman who is given to strife. She's the type of person who thrives on stirring up hornets' nests and doesn't give up the fight until she's swatted every last hornet. And she always seems to manage to get in the last word. Like a continual drip ... drip ... drip, she drives you up a wall and out the window.

┌─ *Some Personal Application* ─────────────────────────────

I'll try to wrap this brick in velvet, but the hard truth is, many contentious daughters are that way because they have contentious mothers. Now wait! Before you throw the brick back—

all things being equal, like begets like. We *do* reproduce after our kind. Pick up the mirror in James 1:19. What do you see? A person that is "quick to hear, slow to speak and slow to anger"? Look harder. Is that you? Because if you're *slow* to hear, *quick* to speak, and *quick* to anger—you're looking a lot like a contentious person. And *guess who* is going to mirror that image? You guessed it—your daughter. Fortunately, there is another side to the mirror—the woman of Proverbs 11:

A gracious woman attains honor. (v. 16a)

To be gracious means "to show favor." It is a picture of the person who is accepting and appreciative. The characteristic is most commonly used in reference to God:

The Lord is compassionate and gracious,
Slow to anger and abounding in lovingkindness.
(Ps. 103:8)

Mirror graciousness to your daughter, clearly and consistently, and glimpse by glimpse she will become a changed person. And someday, she will attain honor as a gracious woman.

Living Insights

Study One

The most famous biblical description of a woman is found in the last chapter of Proverbs. This would be a very appropriate occasion to give this passage careful attention . . . whether you're a woman or a man.

- In an earlier study, we used the technique of paraphrasing. Let's once again tap into this vital resource for personal Bible study. Take Proverbs 31:10–31 and put the twenty-two verses into your own words. Work hard to allow your paraphrase to reflect your own personal understanding of each phrase. Make it an excellent work!

Continued on next page

📖 Living Insights

In our previous study, we did some personal work in Proverbs 31. Now it's time to personalize it even further.

● Based on your study of Proverbs 31:10–31, see if you can identify twenty-two characteristics of excellent womanhood. Copy the chart below and list the qualities in the left-hand column. If you are a woman, use the third column to give yourself a personal evaluation for each quality. Be honest and objective. If you're a man, think of the woman closest to you (wife, daughter, mother, friend . . .) and place a check (√) by the traits best demonstrated by this woman. Make an opportunity to communicate this to her . . . soon!

Proverbs 31:10–31: The Excellent Woman			
Character Trait	Reference	Personal Evaluation	√

You and Your Daughter
(Part Two)
Selected Proverbs

Dale Evans Rogers has written several books of interest about her family and life. In one, in a chapter titled "What Is a Girl?" she gives a tender description of a daughter:

Little girls are the nicest things that happen to people. . . . A girl is Innocence playing in the mud, Beauty standing on its head, Motherhood dragging a doll by the foot. God borrows from many creatures to make a girl. . . . He uses the song of the bird, the squeal of a pig, the stubbornness of the mule, the antics of a monkey, the spryness of a grasshopper, the curiosity of a cat, the speed of a gazelle, the slyness of a fox, the softness of a kitten. . . . She is the loudest when you are thinking, the prettiest when she has provoked you, the busiest at bedtime, the quietest when you want to show her off, and the most flirtatious when she absolutely must not get the best of you again. . . . Who else can cause you more grief, joy, irritation, satisfaction, embarrassment, and genuine delight than this combination of Eve, Salome, and Florence Nightingale?"[1]

Some of you reading this description have young daughters and are probably nodding in agreement. Others of you with older daughters may be leaning back in your chair and saying, "You just wait." For some, raising daughters can be a delight; for others, a disaster. How the experience turns out for you depends upon the qualities that are being built into your daughter's life right now. As a follow-up to the previous study, we'll examine two more contrasting types of women: sensuous and virtuous, indiscreet and godly.

I. Sensuous Woman or Virtuous

These days, the sensuous woman seems to be riding the crest of a Madison Avenue wave while the virtuous woman sits alone on the beach. But one day those waves will come crashing upon the shoals, and the undercurrent of her illicit actions will sweep the sensuous woman into the depths.

A. The sensuous woman. Proverbs 2:16 describes the sexually promiscuous woman as the *strange woman.* The term means "estranged, alienated." She is estranged from a healthy society and outside the circle of proper relationships. The following passages peel away her smooth veneer and allow us to see her as she really is:

1. Dale Evans Rogers, *Time Out, Ladies!* (Westwood, N.J.: Fleming H. Revell Co., 1966), pp. 55–56.

To deliver you from the strange woman,
From the adulteress who flatters with her words;
That leaves the companion of her youth,
And forgets the covenant of her God;
For her house sinks down to death,
And her tracks lead to the dead;
None who go to her return again,
Nor do they reach the paths of life.
(Prov. 2:16–19)
For the lips of an adulteress drip honey,
And smoother than oil is her speech;
But in the end she is bitter as wormwood,
Sharp as a two-edged sword.
Her feet go down to death,
Her steps lay hold of Sheol.
She does not ponder the path of life;
Her ways are unstable, she does not know it.
(5:3–6)
For the commandment is a lamp, and the teaching
  is light;
And reproofs for discipline are the way of life,
To keep you from the evil woman,
From the smooth tongue of the adulteress.
Do not desire her beauty in your heart,
Nor let her catch you with her eyelids.
For on account of a harlot one is reduced to a loaf
  of bread,
And an adulteress hunts for the precious life.
(6:23–26)
And behold, a woman comes to meet him,
Dressed as a harlot and cunning of heart.
She is boisterous and rebellious;
Her feet do not remain at home.
(7:10–11)

Your daughter may never run off into the barren wilderness of a sexually promiscuous life. However, she may be wandering precariously close to its borders if you can see emerging in her some qualities which are embedded in the strange woman of Proverbs.

Some Personal Application

Take this composite of the adulterous woman and place it beside a picture of your daughter. See any comparisons? Is your daughter overly interested in external beauty? Does the way she dress hint at seduction? Listen to your daughter's conversations. Is she given to verbal flattery? Do her words entice or persuade? Examine her attitudes. Is she rebellious? Does she hate to be at home and take every opportunity to get out of the house? If so, take these warning signs to heart and plan to take some positive steps. A growing daughter needs warmth, affection, and communication—especially from her father. She needs smiles and hugs and reassurances of your love. She needs candid talks on life, on what a man looks for in a woman, and on what the Bible says about inner and outer beauty (cf. 1 Pet. 3:3–4). Fathers, you can lose your daughters by default, simply by not being there—or if there, by being silent and passive. Instead of taking a step back in rejection, take a step forward in acceptance—and give her the biggest hug, the warmest smile, and the most sincere "I love you" that you possibly can. Assure her of your love often enough, and those messages will start transforming her from the inside out.

B. The virtuous woman. The type of woman every man wants as a wife is found in Proverbs 31:10–31. As you read, sponge up every word, every character quality, every feminine charm. This is *God's* total woman—excellent, rare, valued above jewels.

An excellent wife, who can find?
For her worth is far above jewels.
The heart of her husband trusts in her,
And he will have no lack of gain.
She does him good and not evil
All the days of her life.
She looks for wool and flax,
And works with her hands in delight.
She is like merchant ships;
She brings her food from afar.
She rises also while it is still night,
And gives food to her household,
And portions to her maidens.
She considers a field and buys it;
From her earnings she plants a vineyard.
She girds herself with strength,
And makes her arms strong.
She senses that her gain is good;
Her lamp does not go out at night.
She stretches out her hands to the distaff,
And her hands grasp the spindle.

She extends her hand to the poor;
And she stretches out her hands to the needy.
She is not afraid of the snow for her household,
For all her household are clothed with scarlet.
She makes coverings for herself;
Her clothing is fine linen and purple.
Her husband is known in the gates,
When he sits among the elders of the land.
She makes linen garments and sells them,
And supplies belts to the tradesmen.
Strength and dignity are her clothing,
And she smiles at the future.
She opens her mouth in wisdom,
And the teaching of kindness is on her tongue.
She looks well to the ways of her household,
And does not eat the bread of idleness.
Her children rise up and bless her;
Her husband also, and he praises her, saying:
"Many daughters have done nobly,
But you excel them all."
Charm is deceitful and beauty is vain,
But a woman who fears the Lord, she shall be praised.
Give her the product of her hands,
And let her works praise her in the gates.

Some Personal Application

A wise woman makes for a jewel of an excellent wife. Proverbs 31:10–31 holds this jewel high in the shimmering light to shine as the perfect role model for every young girl growing up. In the light of this passage, this woman's finely cut facets sparkle brilliantly; she is trustworthy, diligent, committed to the family's well-being, prudent, generous, strong, has integrity, speaks wisely, is kind, and is appreciated by her family. As a life assignment, begin using Proverbs 31:10–31 as a prayer list for your daughter. It's the best way to begin to get a diamond in the rough out of the rough!

II. Indiscreet Woman or Godly

Beauty is only skin deep, as the following proverbs affirm.

A. The indiscreet woman. A woman with discretion is praised (1 Sam. 25:32–33) while a woman without discretion is characterized in almost comic description:

As a ring of gold in a swine's snout,
So is a beautiful woman who lacks discretion.
(Prov. 11:22)

The word *discretion* comes from the Hebrew word meaning "to taste." "The primary meaning of the root is 'to try, or to evaluate, with the tongue, normally with a view to consumption if the flavor is suitable' "[2] (cf. 1 Sam. 14:29, Ps. 34:8). *Discretion* carries the idea of discriminating taste. It is the ability to choose between the tasteful and the tasteless, the appropriate and the inappropriate, right and wrong. A woman lacking that ability, no matter how beautiful, becomes as repulsive as the runny nose of a pig. And her physical beauty, like the gold ring, seems totally out of place.

B. The godly woman. A more pleasing image is the woman of discretion in Proverbs 31. She has tasted both inner and outer beauty—and has chosen as her food that which nourishes the inner self:

Charm is deceitful and beauty is vain,
But a woman who fears the Lord, she shall be praised.
(Prov. 31:30)

The *woman who fears the Lord* realizes that *charm is deceitful* and that *beauty is vain.* She has discriminating taste when it comes to the important and the trivial, the eternal and the temporary.

Some Personal Application

First Peter 3:3–4 provides some excellent advice to every young woman:

> And let not your adornment be merely external braiding the hair, and wearing gold jewelry, or putting on dresses; but let it be the hidden person of the heart, with the imperishable quality of a gentle and quiet spirit, which is precious in the sight of God.

Like all of us, your daughter is constantly being bombarded with messages from our culture that physical beauty is everything for a woman. Almost every magazine, every commercial, every billboard, every movie communicates that message, either explicitly or implicitly. And unless you get close enough to your daughter to whisper in her ear what is precious in God's sight, she may never get the message.

Continued on next page

2. *Theological Wordbook of the Old Testament,* ed. R. Laird Harris, Gleason L. Archer, Jr., and Bruce K. Waltke (Chicago: Moody Press, 1980), vol. 1, p. 351.

🌸 Living Insights

Study One ━━━

In the first part of "You and Your Daughter," we used our Living Insights to examine the characteristics of the excellent woman in Proverbs 31. Many times we can learn even more by providing a point of *contrast*. In understanding the lifestyle of the *strange woman*, we can better appreciate the qualities of the excellent woman.

- Copy the following chart into your notebook. The five passages listed deal with the strange woman. Look for characteristics that specifically identify this type of woman and write them in the middle column. If time permits, refer back to your chart on the excellent woman and try to identify six or more contrasts.

The Strange Woman		
References	Character Traits	Contrasts
Proverbs 2:16–19		
5:1–4		
6:24–35		
7:6–27		
9:13–18		

🌸 Living Insights

Study Two ━━━

You and your daughter will treasure this next assignment for a lifetime. Ask your daughter if she would like to go out with you—for a date. Yes, a real date—dinner, entertainment, the works. Be creative, and go out of your way to make the date relaxed, memorable, and *fun*. No lectures. No correction. No parent-to-child talks. Nothing heavy or intimidating. For an evening, forget you're an adult, and try to get into her world. Music and movies are generally common ground for most children. Try not to pass judgment or offer any unsolicited opinions. Try just listening with a view to gaining a broader understanding of your daughter and of the world she lives in. It would be a treat for her if you shared what you were like when you were her age—how you felt about dating, your worst date, your best date, what movies and music were popular then, how you felt about growing up, how you felt about your parents, and so forth. Make it a scrapbook memory for her—and for you too!

66

You and Your Son

Selected Proverbs

Near the end of the nineteenth century, on the heels of a bloody civil war, Josiah Holland wrote,

God, give us men! A time like this demands
Strong minds, great hearts, true faith and ready hands.[1]

Throughout history, long before the marines, God has been looking for a few good men:

"For the eyes of the Lord move to and fro throughout the earth
that He may strongly support those whose heart is completely
His." (2 Chron. 16:9a)

"And I searched for a man among them who should build up
the wall and stand in the gap before Me." (Ezek. 22:30a)

God, give us men. Give us Noahs, to whom You can trust Your mighty plans; give us Abrahams, who are willing to leave home and homeland to follow Your call; give us Josephs, who would rather endure prison than violate one of Your commands; give us Moseses, who are willing to stand as Your mouthpiece against the most powerful leaders in all the world; give us Daniels, who would rather face a lions' den than compromise their faith; *God, give us men.* However, the reality is that God *does not* give us men—He gives us *boys.* To us, as parents, He gives the task of forging these boys into men. To help equip us for that task, God has provided the book of Proverbs, which is largely the advice of a father to his son. From that advice we will glean five areas of teaching that are essential if our sons will ever grow up to be the few good men God is looking for.

I. Prepare Him for the Times He Must Stand Alone

Proverbs 1:10–16 accents the need to teach our sons the importance of standing up for biblical convictions, even when that means standing alone.

My son, if sinners entice you,
Do not consent.
If they say, "Come with us,
Let us lie in wait for blood,
Let us ambush the innocent without cause;
Let us swallow them alive like Sheol,
Even whole, as those who go down to the pit;
We shall find all kinds of precious wealth,
We shall fill our houses with spoil;
Throw in your lot with us,
We shall all have one purse,"

---

1. Josiah Gilbert Holland, "God, Give Us Men!" in *The Best Loved Poems of the American People,* selected by Hazel Felleman (Garden City, N.Y.: Garden City Books, 1936), p. 132.

My son, do not walk in the way with them.
Keep your feet from their path,
For their feet run to evil,
And they hasten to shed blood.

Notice the three commands: *Do not consent* (v. 10), *do not walk in [their] way* (v. 15), and *keep your feet from their path* (v. 15). Essentially, the father is saying that if the crowd strays from God's path, then follow the path and not the crowd—even if that means following it alone. Your child's peer group exerts a relentless pressure to conform and follow the pack. So if pointing out the right path isn't enough, perhaps a change in peer groups is necessary:

He who walks with wise men will be wise,
But the companion of fools will suffer harm.
(Prov. 13:20)

Moldy bread has a way of spreading its degenerative spores to all the other slices in the loaf—especially when they're bunched together in the hothouse of a plastic bread-bag. So too, your son's companions can have an unbelievable impact on him. As a general rule, sons become like the boys they spend time with.

Some Personal Application

Raising a strongly principled son does not preclude him from having friendships with others. It may, however, necessitate a decision to change the crowd of friends with which he presently associates. This can be a painful experience for the child, but there are two things you can do to help him come to the decision to do that himself. *First,* teach him what a good friend really is. In light of this, have him evaluate the friendships he has. Then have him set his sights on the type of friends he would like to have. *Second,* remind him of the consequences of wrong. Psalm 73 does a good job teaching us not to envy wrongdoers but to consider the consequences of their actions:

But as for me, my feet came close to stumbling;
My steps had almost slipped.
For I was envious of the arrogant,
As I saw the prosperity of the wicked.
(Ps. 73:2–3)
Until I came into the sanctuary of God;
Then I perceived their end. (v. 17)

Since children are young and impressionable, showing them the end result of wrong behavior is essential for them to be able to withstand the magnetic pull which their peer group exerts over them.

II. Teach Him to Be Open to God's Counsel

Along with the ability to stand alone, our sons need to learn what is involved in being open to God's counsel and reproof. Proverbs 3:11–12 talks about this sensitivity to instruction:

> My son, do not reject the discipline of the Lord,
> Or loathe His reproof,
> For whom the Lord loves He reproves,
> Even as a father, the son in whom he delights.

A tender heart toward God is one of the hallmarks of manhood. David, the great warrior who is described to be as fierce as "a bear robbed of her cubs" (2 Sam. 17:8) is also described as " ' "a man after My heart, who will do all My will" ' " (Acts 13:22). David was sensitive and open to God's counsel.

Some Personal Application

How do you develop sensitivity into the life of your son? First of all, *teach him how to respond to your counsel* (cf. Prov. 1:8–9, 3:1–4, 4:1–4, 7:1–3). If he treasures your counsel, then to treasure God's counsel in his adulthood will be an easy transition. Second, *help him see the value of other people's correction.* If he learns to respect the correction of his teacher, coach, employer, and others around him, it will be a natural response to respect God's correction later on in his life. Third, *share the experiences of your life with him.* Share both the positive and the negative and what you learned from them. Fourth, *spend sufficient time counseling your son.* Remember, you're not molding tin soldiers for the dime store—you're forging great men for God! And that takes time.

III. Teach Him How to Deal with Temptation

Interestingly enough, there are only two areas of temptation mentioned specifically in Proverbs: the temptation aroused by the opposite sex and the temptation of food and strong drink.

A. Sexual temptation. With regard to sexual temptation, Proverbs 5:1–5 advises:

> My son, give attention to my wisdom,
> Incline your ear to my understanding;
> That you may observe discretion,
> And your lips may reserve knowledge.
> For the lips of an adulteress drip honey,
> And smoother than oil is her speech;
> But in the end she is bitter as wormwood,
> Sharp as a two-edged sword.

Her feet go down to death,
Her steps lay hold of Sheol.

As parents, we must extol the lush, Edenic beauty of romantic, marital love (Song of Solomon) and explain the dangers of the forbidden fruit of sexual relationships outside of marriage (Prov. 5:1–5). As in Eden, temptation comes from the center of the garden—our heart (Matt. 5:28). Whether your son is a victor or victim of lust is determined on the daily battlefield of his heart. Furthermore, your son needs to realize that overcoming temptation is a continual battle of the flesh (Rom. 6–8).

B. Temptation to excessive indulgence. With regard to food and drink, Proverbs has some pointed advice:

Listen, my son, and be wise,
And direct your heart in the way.
Do not be with heavy drinkers of wine,
Or with gluttonous eaters of meat;
For the heavy drinker and the glutton will come to
poverty,
And drowsiness will clothe a man with rags.
(Prov. 23:19–21)

Verses 29–35 finish the discussion on the dangers of overindulgence and the dangers of letting the search for pleasure dominate your life. If you become its slave, it becomes a harsh and exacting taskmaster.

IV. Teach Him How to Handle Money

The subject of finances covers four areas: teaching a boy how to *give,* how to *earn,* how to *spend,* and how to *save.* He should learn to honor the Lord with his income by making *giving* number one on his priority list (Prov. 3:9–10), especially giving to the poor (Prov. 22:9). In order to do this, the boy must first learn some skill with which he can derive an income (cf. Eph. 4:28, 1 Thess. 4:11, 2 Thess. 3:6–13). How he should wisely spend and invest his money is exemplified in the woman of Proverbs 31 (especially vv. 14, 16, 21, 24). Finally, the principle of saving is best seen in Solomon's illustration of the ant in Proverbs 6:6–8.

V. Teach Him the Value of Hard Work

Two passages from Proverbs underscore the value of hard work:

Poor is he who works with a negligent hand,
But the hand of the diligent makes rich.
He who gathers in summer is a son who acts wisely,
But he who sleeps in harvest is a son who acts shamefully.
(Prov. 10:4–5)
The soul of the sluggard craves and gets nothing,
But the soul of the diligent is made fat. (13:4)

In a nutshell, hard work pays off. Hard, diligent work also pays off in raising your son. After years of planting, watering, weeding, nourishing, and patient waiting, the harvest of your diligence will be evident in your relationship with your son. And if you have led your son to walk with God's Son, your barns will then be truly full, and you, of all people, will be most prosperous.

Living Insights

Study One

The word *son* or *sons* is mentioned over forty times in the book of Proverbs. Are you ready to take a look at *all of them?*

- The chart below lists all the references to *son* in Proverbs. Look up each verse and jot down a word or two of summary. Work briskly, but allow the truth of each passage to sink in.

Sons in Proverbs					
Verses	Summaries	Verses	Summaries	Verses	Summaries
1:1		6:3		19:26	
1:8		6:20		19:27	
1:10		7:1		20:7	
1:15		7:24		23:15	
2:1		8:4		23:19	
3:1		8:31		23:24	
3:11		8:32		23:26	
3:12		10:1		24:13	
3:21		10:5		24:21	
4:1		13:1		27:11	
4:3		13:24		28:7	
4:10		15:20		29:17	
4:20		17:2		29:21	
5:1		17:6		30:1	
5:7		17:25		30:4	
5:20		19:13		31:2	
6:1		19:18			

Continued on next page

🖐 *Living Insights*

Our children are our legacy. As a parent, are you taking that thought seriously? If you still have a son living in your home, let's review some of the practical areas in this study and seek to apply them.

- Below are the five areas of training for our sons. Rate yourself in regard to how you *communicate these* to your boy, with 5 being the best score, and 1 being the worst.

Standing Alone				
1	2	3	4	5

Accepting God's Reproof				
1	2	3	4	5

Dealing with Temptation				
1	2	3	4	5

Handling Finances				
1	2	3	4	5

Working Hard				
1	2	3	4	5

Now, develop an action plan to boost the scores that were lower than the others.

- We have also included two essential ingredients for *parenting* a son. Evaluate yourself in these areas as you did on the previous page.

Consistent Discipline				
1	2	3	4	5

Constant Delight				
1	2	3	4	5

How will you ensure that these qualities will remain balanced?

Seeds a Mother Plants
Selected Scripture

There is no other word that evokes more emotion or prompts more memories than the word *mother.* Memories that time, distance, and even death itself cannot erase. Emotions that still echo like playful children's shouts through the marbled halls in some museum of antiquity. When we think of Mother, images rush to fill our mental screen: rocking-chair laps, storybook mornings, cookies fresh out of the oven. We recall how she doted over us when we were sick, serving chicken soup and crackers on a special tray and pampering us with freshly washed sheets, smelling of sunshine. Like cluttered attics, our minds are crowded with memories of her. Of course, not all childhood memories are pleasant. But of those that are, many probably revolve around a woman who had a way of softening the sharp corners of life—a woman who was many things to many people, but to you she was "Mom." In this lesson we want to look at the seeds which these special women plant in the lives of their children.

I. The Background to 2 Timothy

The letter of 2 Timothy will be the basis for our study, and in it we'll see the blossoming of the seeds planted by a New Testament mother. As the letter opens, Paul is at the end of his life, shackled in a dark, stone-cold prison. Stuffy and repugnant with fetid odors, the dank dungeon reeks with the ominous scent of his impending death. Yet, it is here that Paul pens one of his warmest, most personal letters. The opening verses indicate the close relationship Paul had with Timothy and set a nostalgic tone for the letter:

> Paul, an apostle of Christ Jesus by the will of God, according to the promise of life in Christ Jesus, to Timothy, my beloved son: Grace, mercy and peace from God the Father and Christ Jesus our Lord. I thank God, whom I serve with a clear conscience the way my forefathers did, as I constantly remember you in my prayers night and day. (1:1–3)

Timothy was Paul's *beloved son* (v. 2). We know from Acts 16:1 that Timothy was the son of a Jewish woman who was a believer and a Greek man who was probably not a believer. Therefore, we understand that Paul is addressing Timothy in the spiritual sense; that is, as his spiritual son whom he has nurtured and discipled in the faith. So special was this "son" to Paul that even in his last days, he remembered Timothy in his prayers *night and day* (v. 3).

II. Seeds Planted by Timothy's Mother

In the following verses we see emerging a potential forest of qualities from seeds planted years earlier by Timothy's mother.

A. Transparent tenderness. One quality about Timothy that Paul recalls as he's writing is the young man's tenderness:

> ... longing to see you, even as I recall your tears, so
> that I may be filled with joy. (1:4)

Timothy was not afraid to show emotion, and apparently such emotion as made an indelible imprint on Paul's memory. Tenderness like this is cultivated by example rather than by precept. And, most often, due to cultural influences, it is the example of the mother, as opposed to the father, that produces tenderness in a child.

By Way of Application

Our culture is constantly sending the message that *big boys don't cry;* they are to *be tough, not tender.* The mistake our culture makes is seeing toughness and tenderness as mutually exclusive qualities. Two of history's "manliest" men, David and Jesus, displayed moments of great tenderness. David weeps openly with Jonathan in 1 Samuel 20:41 and repeatedly throughout the Psalms (6:6, 69:10). Jesus weeps over the death of his friend Lazarus (John 11:35) and over the unrepentant city of Jerusalem (Luke 19:41). How often do your children see you being vulnerable and tender? If they don't see those qualities in you, where will they learn them?

B. Authentic Christianity. A second seed that Timothy's mother planted in him was genuine faith:

> For I am mindful of the sincere faith within you, which
> first dwelt in your grandmother Lois, and your
> mother Eunice, and I am sure that it is in you as well.
> (2 Tim. 1:5)

The word *sincere* is from the Greek word *anupokritos*, meaning "unhypocritical." His faith had an authentic quality to it—a quality that was first modeled for him by his grandmother and then by his mother. In chapter 3 of the same book, Paul reminds Timothy that he is surrounded by fakes, phonies, and charlatans:

> But evil men and impostors will proceed from bad
> to worse, deceiving and being deceived. (v. 13)

But Paul goes on to exhort the young Timothy to continue in the faith which he learned in his childhood:

> You, however, continue in the things you have learned
> and become convinced of, knowing from whom you
> have learned them; and that from childhood you have
> known the sacred writings which are able to give you

the wisdom that leads to salvation through faith
which is in Christ Jesus. (vv. 14–15)

In our fast-food, hurry-up world, we try to produce authentic
faith overnight through weekend retreats and seminars. But the
type of genuine faith Timothy had did not spring up overnight.
It was cultivated over the years—at home.

Inspecting the Crops

What are you cultivating in your home—authentic faith or
artificial fruit? Fake fruit may be pleasing to the eye, but
it lacks the taste and nourishment of real fruit, and also
lacks the seeds necessary to reproduce itself. Artificial fruit
may be produced overnight, but authentic faith is homegrown over a lifetime.

C. Inner confidence. The third seed relates to Timothy's self-
esteem:

And for this reason I remind you to kindle afresh the
gift of God which is in you through the laying on of
my hands. For God has not given us a spirit of
timidity, but of power and love and discipline. (1:6–7)

Paul reminds a probably somewhat intimidated Timothy about
two very important things. Namely, that the gift he has is "of
God" and that God has given him not "a spirit of timidity, but
of power and love and discipline." Here Paul exhorts Timothy
to fan the embers of his neglected gift, and he does so by
appealing to his strengths. The text is clear that Timothy's
spiritual gift came through Paul's ministry (v. 6), but the power,
love, and self-control that were sourced in God undoubtedly
were transmitted through Timothy's roots (see 2 Tim. 3:15–17).

A Principle for Building Confidence

A primary way to build self-esteem in children is to equip
them with strengths which they can draw from in times of
weakness. Obviously, at the time of Paul's writing, Timothy
was going through a period of withdrawal (1:6) that was
the result of something he feared (v. 7). Instead of focusing
on the negative and being critical, Paul gives him positive
encouragement that is based on certain strengths which
Timothy had within him. Are you equipping your children
with strengths they can draw on in times of weakness? Do
you brow-beat them when they are negligent or fearful of
their responsibilities, or do you encourage them by emphasizing their strengths?

D. Demonstrative love. In verse 7 of 2 Timothy 1, the word *love* is *agapē* in the original language and carries with it the idea of unselfishness. There is in this word the demonstrative sense of reaching out and doing something for the highest good of another. And where is that type of loved learned? Where does the child see *agapē* love in the flesh? In a mother who, without complaint, gets up at all hours of the night to attend to a sick child . . . in a mother who tirelessly bakes and cleans and sews so another may be fed and refreshed and clothed . . . in a mother who goes the extra mile past boredom to read for the hundredth time the child's favorite storybook with first-time enthusiasm. No one wears the fabric of selfless love quite as naturally, as purely, and as elegantly as a mother.

E. Self-control. A spirit of *discipline* or *self-control* is another seed which had been deposited in Timothy's life (2 Tim. 1:7). Self-control, the last of the fruit of the Spirit listed in Galatians 5:23, doesn't blossom in a child at maturity. It is not spontaneously generated. The seed must be planted early in life. Discipline must start young and be diligently and lovingly cultivated over the years if the child is ever to internalize that discipline and translate it into self-control.

A Thought for the Road

A mother's heart is the schoolroom where the child learns the ABCs of life—where tenderness is translated into all its subtle nuances, where faith is multiplied, where confidence is read aloud, where love is conjugated into all its tenses, and where self-discipline stands as monitor. And this is why it is said that "one good mother is worth a hundred school masters."[1]

Continued on next page

---

1. George Herbert, quoted in *Speaker's Encyclopedia of Stories, Quotations, and Anecdotes,* ed. Jacob M. Braude (Englewood Cliffs, N.J.: Prentice Hall, 1966), p. 266.

Living Insights

Study One ━━━━━━━━━━━━━━━━━━━━━━━━━━━━━━━━━━━━

Timothy's mother planted at least five specific seeds of character into her son which attracted Paul (and others) to that young man. Each of those traits are noble ones and deserving of more study.

- Copy the following chart into your notebook. Using an exhaustive concordance or one in the back of your Bible, look up the five words in the chart. Check out the Scripture references and write a summary of each passage. Your five short "topical studies" will give you expanded information on these important character traits.

Seeds a Mother Plants		
Seeds	Scriptures	Summaries
Tenderness		
Godliness		
Confidence		
Love		
Self-control		

Living Insights

Study Two ━━━━━━━━━━━━━━━━━━━━━━━━━━━━━━━━━━━━

We have digested a large amount of material in these messages! In our final study we'll take the time to review, but for now let's think back through the lessons prayerfully.

- Let's use our Living Insights section to talk with God. Begin by thanking the Lord for what He has taught you through this study. As you think back over the lessons, thank Him for the encouragement you received in areas of strength. Then, turn your attention to those topics that need some work. Ask for His help in bringing these trouble spots into their proper position in your life. Use this time as a period of confession, thanksgiving, petition, and worship.

Dads, Front and Center
Selected Scripture

In her excellent essay titled "What Is a Father?" Edith Schaeffer writes:

Unhappily, the word *father* has a garbled sense to many people of this century. It needs redefinition—not just in words, but in understanding and in day-by-day life. People may shiver a bit or stiffen up inside when you say that God is a Father to us. Often the word *father* has a negative emotion connected with it that has grown out of thinking of *father* as the definition of a person with whom there is no communication, who cannot understand one's thoughts, feelings, or actions, and who must be avoided or from whom one must run away. Without realizing it, people transfer to God the imperfections and even the sins of earthly fathers they have known. Even Christians often portray the very opposite qualifications to what a father is supposed to be, and give their children a warped response to the word.[1]

Some of us have come from homes where the father was solid, reliable, and practical. He was there whenever we needed him. Some have come from homes where the father was visionary and creative, full of life and wonder. Others have come from homes where the father was impatient, angry, and even brutal. Some come from homes where the father was shiftless and lazy. Some have workaholics for fathers. Some have alcoholics. Some have fathers who have never grown up. Some have fathers that seem to have never been young. Whatever kind of father we had, most likely our concept of God as a father will be affected by how we perceive our earthly fathers. And that is the sobering responsibility of fatherhood—that fathers are to mirror the image of God Himself. Distortions about God exist, at least in part, because too many fathers are like the twisted mirrors we see in carnival fun houses. With each bend in the mirror, the reflection of God as Father becomes more and more distorted to the child. In this lesson, we will examine the qualities of a caring father as they are reflected in the life of Paul, in hopes that we, as fathers, can straighten out the bends that exist in our own lives. Then, as the moon reflects the sun, so we shall reflect our Heavenly Father to our children.

I. Five Traits of a Good Father

While in Thessalonica, Paul gave himself to the church, laboring diligently to pour his life into the people there. After he left, he received news about the waves of persecution and the disturbance that was troubling the Thessalonian church. In response, he attempted to buttress their faith by first sending them Timothy. Then, when Timothy returned with his report on how the church fared,

---

1. Edith Schaeffer, *A Way of Seeing* (Old Tappan, N.J.: Fleming H. Revell Co., 1977), pp. 24–25.

Paul wrote them the endearing letter of love, exhortation, and instruction which we know as 1 Thessalonians. As we look at chapter 2, we feel the heartbeat of strong emotion from a loving father. In verse 7, he states that he was "gentle among [them], as a nursing mother tenderly cares for her own children." Skipping down to verse 11, Paul says he had been "imploring each one of [them] as a father would his own children." The descriptions *as a mother* and *as a father* appear nowhere else in Paul's writings. In using these dual images, Paul communicates his parental care and concern for the church. And, it is from the verses surrounded by these tenderly cupped parental hands that we will derive five traits of a good father.

A. A fond affection. Paul begins verse 8 with the words, "Having thus a fond affection for you."[2] The picture is one of a father holding a child tenderly and feeling himself affectionately drawn to the little one. In the story of the prodigal son in Luke 15, we see the *fond affection* of a father upon the return of his wayward son:

> "And he got up and came to his father. But while he was still a long way off, his father saw him, and felt compassion for him, and ran and embraced him, and kissed him." (v. 20)

A Time to Embrace

Affection in the home should be visible as well as vocal. The communication of acceptance and approval is transmitted most effectively to children through the nonverbal display of affection: touching, embracing, kissing, holding hands, sitting them on your lap. In Mark 1:40–41, Jesus sensitively reaches out to touch one of society's untouchables:

> And a leper came to Him, beseeching Him and falling on his knees before Him, and saying to Him, "If You are willing, You can make me clean." And moved with compassion, He stretched out His hand, and touched him, and said to him, "I am willing; be cleansed."

---

2. The phrase "a fond affection" is the translation of the Greek word *homeiromai*. This word is used nowhere else in the New Testament. It is used, however, a few times outside the New Testament. For example, the word occurs on a burial inscription in reference to parents mourning the loss of their son where it means "with intense longing" *(Theological Dictionary of the New Testament,* ed. Gerhard Kittel and Gerhard Friedrich [Grand Rapids, Mich.: William B. Eerdmans Publishing Co., 1973], vol. 5, p. 176). Moulton and Milligan suggest the word is "a term of endearment . . . borrowed from the language of the nursery" (James Hope Moulton and George Milligan, *The Vocabulary of the Greek New Testament* [Grand Rapids, Mich.: William B. Eerdmans Publishing Co., 1972], p. 447).

Jesus could have healed the man with only the words "I am willing; be cleansed," but compassion moved Him to stretch out His hand and *touch* the man. The leper had probably not felt the physical touch of affection since he had developed the dreaded disease. Jesus reached out to someone who felt he was on the outside of life—and with His touch drew him in. If Jesus dared to reach out and touch a leper, certainly we should dare to reach out and, with affection, touch our children and draw them in with arms of acceptance and approval.

B. A transparent life. The second trait of a good father is found in the next portion of 1 Thessalonians 2:8:

> Having thus a fond affection for you, we were well-pleased to impart to you not only the gospel of God but also our own lives, because you had become very dear to us.

A recipe, to be inviting, needs to be more than just a printed page in a cookbook. It needs to be meticulously prepared, exquisitely arranged, and displayed in full color. Paul not only passed on to the Thessalonians the black and white of the gospel message but allowed them to sample the incarnation of that message in his own life. He placed himself on their table, visible to all. That's a transparent life.

Breathing Life into Our Words

Children perceive life in concrete terms rather than in the abstract. The younger the children are, the truer this is. This is why children's books start out as picture books. As children grow older, words accompany the pictures in their books. As they reach adulthood, they are weaned to reading books that have all print and no pictures. To younger children, the abstract concepts of the gospel—love, atonement, repentance, reconciliation—slip like Jell-O through the grasp of their tiny, mental fingers. But these abstractions become concrete as your children observe your life—when you make it transparent to them. And, if your life is a full-color picture of Christ, it will invite them to feast on the words of the gospel.

C. An unselfish diligence. Verse 9 reveals another trait of a good father:

> For you recall, brethren, our labor and hardship, how working night and day so as not to be a burden to any of you, we proclaimed to you the gospel of God.

To the Thessalonians, Paul's life was a picture of hard work—*labor and hardship*; diligent work—*working night and day*; and unselfish work—*so as not to be a burden to any of you.* One of the most important slices of your life to serve to your child is an *unselfish diligence.* Fatherhood is a difficult act—constantly juggling the responsibilities of work, home, and church, trying to keep them all in the air without dropping any. It's often hectic, with not enough time for each responsibility and practically none for yourself. To do it successfully requires a lot of hard, diligent, and unselfish work.

D. A spiritual authenticity. Verse 10 sketches the lines of a fourth trait of a good father:

> You are witnesses, and so is God, how devoutly and uprightly and blamelessly we behaved toward you believers.

Paul's life had spiritual authenticity. He behaved *devoutly, uprightly,* and *blamelessly.* The word *devoutly* highlights "religious piety"[3] and describes a person devoted to God's service. The word *uprightly* has a slightly different shade of meaning. Fundamentally, it means "conformity to God's law."[4] So what is in view here is Paul's moral conduct. The final description of his behavior—*blamelessly*—reveals the degree of his devotion to God and the degree of morality in his conduct. Both are without spot or blame. In the first portion of the verse, Paul calls the people at Thessalonica to step forward as *witnesses.* In the rest of the verse, the jury's verdict is that Paul was without blame in his behavior toward the people of the church. Devout, upright, and blameless behavior add up to spiritual authenticity. And the people saw these qualities so clearly that they were called upon to testify as eyewitnesses.

E. A positive influence. Verses 11–12 furnish us with the final trait for our study:

> Just as you know how we were exhorting and encouraging and imploring each one of you as a father would his own children, so that you may walk in a

---

3. Robert L. Thomas, "1 Thessalonians," *The Expositor's Bible Commentary* (Grand Rapids, Mich.: Zondervan Publishing House, 1978), vol. 11, p. 255.

4. Leon Morris, *The First and Second Epistles to the Thessalonians* (Grand Rapids, Mich.: William B. Eerdmans Publishing Co., 1973), p. 83.

manner worthy of the God who calls you into His own kingdom and glory.

A good father exerts a *positive influence* on his children. He *exhorts*. He *encourages*. He *implores*. These are the words Paul uses to describe how a father relates to his children. He doesn't shout. He doesn't demean. He doesn't dictate. He is not a demagogue—he is their dad. And finally, all the exhorting, encouraging, and imploring have one unified, lofty purpose: *so that you may walk in a manner worthy of the God who calls you into His own kingdom and glory.*

┌─ A Concluding Picture ─────────────────────

"We are told that an eagle flies under the baby eaglets in order to catch them if they fall while learning to fly. In this way, God pictures the ready refuge we may expect from Him. He not only is ready to gather us under His wings to shelter us from dangers, but He cares enough to stay close, as the eagle flies directly under, in order to be ready when the moment comes. This is a far cry from the father who waits to pounce upon his child's every mistake and to make the child fear to be anywhere near the father when he falls. God's perfect fatherliness is one of loving care, realizing that falls will come. When is a child to learn that this is what a father is? What pattern is the child to have when he becomes a father—and a new generation is suddenly using the same word *father*—with what connotation?"[5]

Continued on next page

---

5. Edith Schaeffer, *A Way of Seeing*, p. 26.

🌳 Living Insights

Did you realize the Bible had so much to say regarding you and your child? Let's take a few minutes to review what we've learned from God's Word about this process we call parenting.

- After copying the following chart into your notebook, go back over your notes and write down the most important truth you learned from each lesson.

You and Your Child	
Lesson Titles	Important Truths
Knowing Your Child	
Breaking Granddad's Bent	
Loving Your Child	
You Can't Have One without the Other	
Disciplining Your Child	
The Ministry of the Rod	
Training Your Child	
The Home Training of Jesus	
Releasing Your Child	
You and Your Daughter (Part One)	
You and Your Daughter (Part Two)	
You and Your Son	
Seeds a Mother Plants	
Dads, Front and Center	

Living Insights

As James said so well in his New Testament letter, we want to be *doers* of the Word, not just *hearers*. As we review this series, let's turn our attention to the applications we've made.

- The following chart is similar to the previous one, except it focuses on application. Review your Bible, study guide, and notes to determine one important application you made in each lesson.

You and Your Child	
Lesson Titles	Important Applications
Knowing Your Child	
Breaking Granddad's Bent	
Loving Your Child	
You Can't Have One without the Other	
Disciplining Your Child	
The Ministry of the Rod	
Training Your Child	
The Home Training of Jesus	
Releasing Your Child	
You and Your Daughter (Part One)	
You and Your Daughter (Part Two)	
You and Your Son	
Seeds a Mother Plants	
Dads, Front and Center	

Books for Probing Further

It is said that football is a game of inches. Similarly, the gains in parenting are usually made a little at a time. There are few crowd-dazzling runs and fewer still touchdown passes, for essentially, parenting is a lineman's game. It's life in the trenches—sweating and grunting—with little glory. There are too few time-outs, and it's easy to jump offsides. Also, it can be frustrating work. Just when you think you've got your children in line, one of them does an end run. From time to time we all drop the ball as far as our responsibilities to our children go. And through painful experience, we know that those fumbles are often hard to recover. More than once we've wanted to quit and check in the equipment. But it seems just at those times, we get an encouraging word from the coach, or our teammates huddle around us to show their support—and we get a second wind. We hope this series of studies has been that type of encouragement and support. To put a few more plays in your gamebook, we have listed the following books as a final help for you. Happy reading, and all the best for you—and your child.

I. For General Study
Butterworth, Bill. *My Kids Are My Best Teachers.* Old Tappan, N.J.: Fleming H. Revell Co., 1986.

Campbell, Ross. *How to Really Love Your Child.* Wheaton, Ill.: Victor Books, 1984.

Dobson, James. *Hide or Seek.* Old Tappan, N.J.: Fleming H. Revell Co., 1974.

Meier, Paul D. *Christian Child-rearing and Personality Development.* Grand Rapids, Mich.: Baker Book House, 1977.

Narramore, Clyde M. *Parents at Their Best.* Nashville: Thomas Nelson Publishers, 1985.

Smalley, Gary. *The Key to Your Child's Heart.* Waco, Tex.: Word Books, 1984.

Swindoll, Charles R. *You and Your Child.* Nashville: Thomas Nelson Publishers, 1977.

Temple, Joe. *Know Your Child.* Grand Rapids, Mich.: Baker Book House, 1974.

II. For Building Memories
Birkey, Verna. *Building Happy Memories and Family Traditions.* Old Tappan, N.J.: Fleming H. Revell Co., 1980.

Schaeffer, Edith. *What Is a Family?* Old Tappan, N.J.: Fleming H. Revell Co., 1975.

III. For Dads
Lewis, Paul. *Famous Fathers.* Elgin, Ill.: David C. Cook Publishing Co., 1984.

Schaeffer, Edith. "What Is a Father?" in *A Way of Seeing.* Old Tappan, N.J.: Fleming H. Revell Co., 1977.

Shedd, Charlie. *The Best Dad Is a Good Lover.* Kansas City, Kans.: Sheed Andrews and McMeel, Inc., 1977.

IV. For Moms

Fleming, Jean. *A Mother's Heart.* Colorado Springs, Colo.: NavPress, 1984.

Moster, Mary Beth. *When Mom Goes to Work.* Chicago: Moody Press, 1980.

Rushford, Patricia H. *What Kids Need Most in a Mom.* Old Tappan, N.J.: Fleming H. Revell Co., 1986.

V. For Single Parents

Barnes, Robert G. *Single Parenting.* Wheaton, Ill.: Tyndale House Publishers, 1984.

Bustanoby, André. *Being a Single Parent.* Grand Rapids, Mich.: Zondervan Publishing Co., 1985.

VI. For Your Child's Spiritual Growth

Hendrichsen, Walter A. *How to Disciple Your Child.* Wheaton, Ill.: Victor Books, 1981.

Narramore, Bruce. *An Ounce of Prevention.* Grand Rapids, Mich.: Zondervan Publishing Co., 1971.

VII. For Disciplining Your Child

Dobson, James. *Dare to Discipline.* Wheaton, Ill.: Tyndale House Publishers, 1970.

——— . *The Strong-Willed Child.* Wheaton, Ill.: Tyndale House Publishers, 1978.

VIII. For Educating Your Child

Hunt, Gladys. *Honey for a Child's Heart.* Grand Rapids, Mich.: Zondervan Publishing Co., 1982.

Jacobs, Leland B., ed. *Using Literature with Young Children.* New York: Teachers College Press, 1978.

Moore, Raymond and Dorothy. *Homegrown Kids.* Waco, Tex.: Word Books, 1981.

Rowen, Dolores. *Ways to Help Them Learn.* Ventura, Calif.: Regal Books, 1974.

IX. For Raising the Adolescent Child

Dobson, James. *Preparing for Adolescence.* Ventura, Calif.: Vision House, 1983.

Kesler, Jay, ed. *Parents and Teenagers.* Wheaton, Ill.: Victor Books, 1984.

Narramore, Bruce. *Adolescence Is Not an Illness.* Old Tappan, N.J.: Fleming H. Revell Co., 1980.

X. For Sex Education

Ketterman, Grace H. *How to Teach Your Child about Sex.* Old Tappan, N.J.: Fleming H. Revell Co., 1981.

White, John. *Eros Defiled.* Downers Grove, Ill.: InterVarsity Press, 1977.

Acknowledgments

Insight for Living is grateful for permission to quote from the following sources:

Rogers, Dale Evans. *Time Out, Ladies!* Westwood, N.J.: Fleming H. Revell Co., 1966.

Schaeffer, Edith. *A Way of Seeing.* Old Tappan, N.J.: Fleming H. Revell Co., 1977.

Swindoll, Charles R. *You and Your Child.* Nashville: Thomas Nelson Publishers, 1977. Because the book and the study guide deal with similar subject matter, the introductory letter has been condensed from the book for this publication.

Chuck is grateful to his friend, Dr. Joe Temple of Abilene, Texas, for passing on his keen insights about rearing children. With his approval, the first two chapters of this series include some of the truths he printed in his book Know Your Child *(Grand Rapids, Mich.: Baker Book House, 1974). We appreciate the publisher's allowing Chuck to use and build upon some of Dr. Temple's original thoughts.*

Equal appreciation goes to Dr. Howard Hendricks, Chuck's major professor at Dallas Theological Seminary, for insights from his course on "The Christian Home." His life convinced Chuck that one can actually practice what he preaches.

Insight for Living
Cassette Tapes
YOU AND YOUR CHILD

In this day of domestic confusion and parent-child conflict, these insights from Scripture are long overdue. Here is direction on many of the techniques you now struggle with as a parent: understanding your children, dealing with their low self-esteem or strong will, disciplining effectively, cultivating a spiritual hunger for God, and handling sibling rivalry. This guidance is all from the Bible—carefully stated, with wisdom and sensitivity underlying its principles. It is a good series to study with a group as well as individually.

			U.S.	Canadian
YYC	CS	Cassette series—includes album cover	$39.50	$50.25
		Individual cassettes—include messages A and B	5.00	6.35

These prices are effective as of July 1986 and are subject to change without notice.

YYC 1-A: *Knowing Your Child*—Proverbs 22:6, Psalm 139
      B: *Breaking Granddad's Bent*—Exodus 34:5-8

YYC 2-A: *Loving Your Child*—Psalms 127-128
      B: *You Can't Have One without the Other*—Selected Proverbs

YYC 3-A: *Disciplining Your Child*—Selected Proverbs
      B: *The Ministry of the Rod*—1 Samuel 2:11-3:13

YYC 4-A: *Training Your Child*—Deuteronomy 6:4-9
      B: *The Home Training of Jesus*—Luke 2, Hebrews 5:8

YYC 5-A: *Releasing Your Child*—Selected Scripture
      B: *You and Your Daughter (Part One)*—Selected Proverbs

YYC 6-A: *You and Your Daughter (Part Two)*—Selected Proverbs
      B: *You and Your Son*—Selected Proverbs

YYC 7-A: *Seeds a Mother Plants*—Selected Scripture
      B: *Dads, Front and Center*—Selected Scripture

Ordering Information

U.S. ordering information: You are welcome to use our toll-free number (for Visa and MasterCard orders only) between the hours of 8:30 A.M. and 4:00 P.M., Pacific time, Monday through Friday. The number is **(800) 772-8888.** This number may be used anywhere in the continental United States excluding California, Hawaii, and Alaska. Orders from those areas are handled through our Sales Department at **(714) 870-9161.** We are unable to accept collect calls.

Your order will be processed promptly. We ask that you allow four to six weeks for delivery by fourth-class mail. If you wish your order to be shipped first-class, please add 10 percent of the total order cost (not including California sales tax) for shipping and handling.

Canadian ordering information: Your order will be processed promptly. We ask that you allow approximately four weeks for delivery by first-class mail to the U.S./Canadian border. All orders will be shipped from our office in Fullerton, California. For our listeners in British Columbia, a 7 percent sales tax must be added to the total of all tape orders (not including first-class postage). For further information, please contact our office at **(604) 272-5811.**

Payment options: We accept personal checks, money orders, Visa, and MasterCard in payment for materials ordered. Unfortunately, we are unable to offer invoicing or COD orders. If the amount of your check or money order is less than the amount of your purchase, your check will be returned so that you may place your order again with the correct amount. All orders must be paid in full before shipment can be made.

Returned checks: There is a $10 charge for any returned check (regardless of the amount of your order) to cover processing and invoicing.

Guarantee: Our tapes are guaranteed for ninety days against faulty performance or breakage due to a defect in the tape. For best results, please be sure your tape recorder is in good operating condition and is cleaned regularly.

Mail your order to one of the following addresses:

Insight for Living
Sales Department
Post Office Box 4444
Fullerton, CA 92634

Insight for Living Ministries
Post Office Box 2510
Vancouver, BC
Canada V6B 3W7

Quantity discounts and gift certificates are available upon request.

Overseas ordering information is provided on the reverse side of the order form.

Order Form

Please send me the following cassette tapes:

The current series: ☐ YYC CS You and Your Child

Individual cassettes: ☐ YYC 1   ☐ YYC 2   ☐ YYC 3   ☐ YYC 4
☐ YYC 5   ☐ YYC 6   ☐ YYC 7

I am enclosing:

$_____ To purchase the cassette series for $39.50 (in Canada $50.25*) which includes the album cover

$_____ To purchase individual tapes at $5.00 each (in Canada $6.35*)

$_____ Total of purchases

$_____ If the order will be received in California, please add 6 percent sales tax

$_____ U.S. residents please add 10 percent for first-class shipping and handling if desired

$_____ *British Columbia residents please add 7 percent sales tax

$_____ Canadian residents please add 6 percent for postage

$_____ **Overseas residents please add appropriate postage** (See postage chart under "Overseas Ordering Information.")

$_____ As a gift to the Insight for Living radio ministry for which a tax-deductible receipt will be issued

$_____ **Total amount due (Please do not send cash.)**

Form of payment:

☐ Check or money order made payable to Insight for Living
☐ Credit card (Visa or MasterCard only)
If there is a balance: ☐ apply it as a donation ☐ please refund

---

Credit card purchases:
☐ Visa   ☐ MasterCard number _____
Expiration date _____
Signature _____
We cannot process your credit card purchase without your signature.

Name _____
Address _____
_____
City _____
State/Province _____ Zip/Postal code _____
Country _____
Telephone (___) _____ Radio Station ___ ___ ___ ___

Should questions arise concerning your order, we may need to contact you.

Overseas Ordering Information

If you do not live in the United States or Canada, please note the following information. This will ensure efficient processing of your request.

Estimated time of delivery: We ask that you allow approximately twelve to sixteen weeks for delivery by surface mail. If you would like your order sent airmail, the length of delivery may be reduced. All orders will be shipped from our office in Fullerton, California.

Payment options: Due to fluctuating currency rates, we can accept only personal checks made payable in U.S. funds, international money orders, Visa, and MasterCard in payment for materials ordered. If the amount of your check or money order is less than the amount of your purchase, your check will be returned so that you may place your order again with the correct amount. All orders must be paid in full before shipment can be made.

Returned checks: There is a $10 charge for any returned check (regardless of the amount of your order) to cover processing and invoicing.

Postage and handling: Please add to the amount of purchase the postage cost for the service you desire. All orders must include postage based on the chart below.

Purchase Amount		Surface Postage	Airmail Postage
From	To	Percentage of Order	Percentage of Order
$ .01	$15.00	40%	75%
15.01	75.00	25%	45%
75.01	or more	15%	40%

Guarantee: Our tapes are guaranteed for ninety days against faulty performance or breakage due to a defect in the tape. For best results, please be sure your tape recorder is in good operating condition and is cleaned regularly.

Mail your order or inquiry to the following address:

Insight for Living
Sales Department
Post Office Box 4444
Fullerton, CA 92634

Quantity discounts and gift certificates are available upon request.